P9-ARF-596

The

HARNEY & SONS

GUIDE *to* TEA

The

HARNEY & SONS

GUIDE *to* TEA

MICHAEL HARNEY

with Emily Kaiser

THE PENGUIN PRESS · *New York* · 2008

THE PENGUIN PRESS
Published by the Penguin Group
Penguin Group (USA) Inc., 375 Hudson Street, New York, New York 10014, U. S. A. • Penguin Group
(Canada), 90 Eglinton Avenue East, Suite 700, Toronto, Ontario, Canada M4P 2Y3 (a division of Pearson
Penguin Canada Inc.) • Penguin Books Ltd, 80 Strand, London WC2R 0RL, England • Penguin Ireland, 25
St. Stephen's Green, Dublin 2, Ireland (a division of Penguin Books Ltd) • Penguin Books Australia Ltd, 250
Camberwell Road, Camberwell, Victoria 3124, Australia (a division of Pearson Australia Group Pty Ltd) •
Penguin Books India Pvt Ltd, 11 Community Centre, Panchsheel Park, New Delhi – 110 017, India •
Penguin Group (NZ), 67 Apollo Drive, Rosedale, North Shore 0632, New Zealand (a division of Pearson
New Zealand Ltd) • Penguin books (South Africa) (Pty) Ltd, 24 Sturdee Avenue, Rosebank,
Johannesburg 2196, South Africa

Penguin Books Ltd, Registered Offices:
80 Strand, London WC2R 0RL, England

First published in 2008 by The Penguin Press,
a member of Penguin Group (USA) Inc.
Copyright © Michael Harney, 2008
All rights reserved

LIBRARY OF CONGRESS CATALOGING IN PUBLICATION DATA
Harney, Michael, date.
The Harney & Sons guide to tea / Michael Harney.
p.   cm.
Includes index.
ISBN 978-1-59420-138-7
1. Tea.   2. Tea tasting.   I. Title.   II. Title: Harney and Sons guide
to tea.   III. Title: Guide to tea.
GT2905.H37 2008
394.1'2—dc22
2008012495

Printed in the United States of America
3   5   7   9   10   8   6   4

Book design and maps by Meighan Cavanaugh

Without limiting the rights under copyright reserved above, no part of this publication may be reproduced, stored
in or introduced into a retrieval system, or transmitted, in any form or by any means (electronic, mechanical,
photocopying, recording or otherwise), without the prior written permission of both the copyright owner and the
above publisher of this book.

The scanning, uploading, and distribution of this book via the Internet or via any other means without the permission of the publisher is illegal and punishable by law. Please purchase only authorized electronic editions and
do not participate in or encourage electronic piracy of copyrightable materials. Your support of the author's rights
is appreciated.

For Brigitte
and the boys

Contents

The

HARNEY & SONS

GUIDE *to* TEA

INTRODUCTION

Over the last twenty years as a tea buyer, blender, and connoisseur, I've seen the landscape change radically for tea lovers. More teas are available today, of a better quality and in a wider range of flavors, than at any point in history. In this new tea world, it seemed to me that tea drinkers needed a more complete guide to the ancient beverage, a handbook to give them a more nuanced and clearer understanding of the drink. As we embark on this tea-tasting journey—from the light honeysuckle of the finest white teas to the rich smokiness of the darkest blacks—you will cultivate your palate and enhance your ability to discern and enjoy tea.

I first encountered tea in 1970, when I was fifteen. My father, John Harney, then ran the White Hart Inn in Salisbury, Connecticut. He had taken on a side project selling loose tea with a neighbor, Stanley Mason. A diminutive, charming Englishman, Mason had started a small mail-order business, Sarum Teas, in our town after many loyal years of service in New York to the British tea firm Brooke Bond. As a teenager, I helped Mason and my father carry heavy wooden chests of tea down to the White Hart basement, where we would package the tea into small tins. The dry black filaments all looked the same to me. I had no idea how anyone could tell them apart or why anyone would want to. In 1983, my father started his own small tea company. He called it Harney & Sons, but that was a misnomer; my brothers and I were involved in our own projects.

Today, three of us run Harney & Sons together: my father, my brother Paul, and myself. I was the first son to sign on in 1988. I first started to change my mind about tea after working in France with Camus Cognac, a family firm that had been making the spirit for several generations. While working with their distillers and blenders, I came to envy their traditions of family and agriculture, their collective pursuit of liquid perfection. I saw a chance to replicate those traditions in tea. Tea is, after all, an even more ancient drink than wine, and one that merits the same understanding. As I took on the roles of buyer and blender in my family's burgeoning tea company, I grew determined to learn what makes tea great.

I have had some spectacular adventures. In search of the world's best teas, I have explored some beautiful country along the tea belt from China and Japan through India and down to Sri Lanka. I have visited some of the flushest tea fields and taken tours of state-of-the-art tea factories as well as some enchantingly simple operations. I have befriended some remarkable tea farmers, manufacturers, and brokers, men with ties to the drink that stretch back centuries. In my work at our factory, whether examining new shipments or checking on our own teas, I taste around eighty teas a day, at least sixteen thousand teas a year. From dozens of journeys, hundreds of queries, and thousands upon thousands of sips of tea, I have mastered enough to know what makes tea so spectacular. The goal of this book is to allow you to achieve the same level of mastery, with far less time and travel.

Twenty years ago, a tea guide was hardly necessary. It was easy enough to become an expert in Earl Grey, English Breakfast, and the other blends that dominated the market. Today, it's a different story. In only the last decade, globalization and economic development have helped widen access to more flavorful teas from among the best tea-producing countries of China, Japan, and India. Small batches of what were long considered local teas are now air-freighted to the West, providing an unprecedented variety of tastes and styles to choose from. The invention of vacuum packaging has allowed these teas to arrive on our shores more fresh and flavorful than ever before.

Adding to tea's popularity, scientists report ever more good news about the drink's health benefits. As a source of antioxidants, tea contains compounds that may help prevent cancer and cardiovascular disease. Research also continues into theanine, a compound in tea that increases concentration and soothes as it stimulates, making tea a milder, more beneficial pick-me-up than coffee or chocolate. *The Wall Street Journal* reports that total U.S. tea sales are nearly four times what they were in 1990, and the tea market is rapidly changing—and expanding—to accommodate new tea drinkers.

From our original six teas, Harney & Sons now sells more than three hundred. A visit to any good tea shop will yield sweet, vegetal green teas from China; Senchas, Banchas, and Hojichas from Japan; fragrant high-mountain oolongs from Taiwan; robust low-grown black teas from Sri Lanka; and three different seasons of tea from Darjeeling.

With so many new options available, how do you choose? How can you judge a good Assam from a bad? A properly brewed Sencha from a weak one? A spring Darjeeling from one harvested in fall? *The Harney & Sons Guide to Tea* will show you how to navigate this more complex tea world. This book is a compendium of the fifty-six best pure teas I think a tea connoisseur ought to know, with guided tasting notes for each.

Let me clarify what I mean by *pure* teas. Pure teas are harvested from the same variety of tea plant, from the same region, and ideally from the same factory. In the tea world, the opposite of pure teas are *blends*. Blends come in one of two forms. Some are teas mixed with other teas, like English Breakfast, a mix of Indian and Chinese teas. Others are teas blended with different ingredients entirely, such as Earl Grey, a black tea scented with bergamot, a type of citrus. I include both English Breakfast and Earl Grey in this book because I consider them ideal starting points to understanding the pure teas that go into them. Much as I enjoy drinking blends (and concocting them for my tea company), their additives can mask the flavor of pure tea. Today, the finest pure teas have nuance, character, and flavor comparable to those of fine wines.

Like the finest wines, pure teas are fundamentally an agricultural product, subject to all the vagaries of Mother Nature. The best tea makers exploit nature to give their teas delicious flavors, artfully manipulating the ways the leaves grow and how they dry into tea. Tea starts its life as bright green leaves on a branch of the evergreen *Camellia sinensis*. These trees can grow to heights of thirty feet or more; they thrive in dappled shade in moist subtropical climates. The white and pink blossoms yield edible (if bitter) small tea nuts. The soft, shiny leaves have finely jagged edges and slightly pointed tips. Fresh-plucked tea leaves make an incredibly bitter brew; only after they have withered and dried do they take on their extraordinary aromas and flavors.

The best teas available today—and with one Kenyan exception, all the teas in this book—come from Asia: China, Japan, and Taiwan, as well as India and Sri Lanka. These countries make the finest teas for a number of reasons, but simply put, they have grown tea the longest and have the most expertise with the plant. The plant is indigenous to China and has grown in that country's Himalayan foothills for thousands of years. China is responsible for the invention not only of green and black teas, but also of white teas, oolongs, and puerhs. Japan has been cultivating green tea since the ninth century. The British did not start drinking black tea until well into the seventeenth century, after Dutch traders first brought black tea to Europe. By the nineteenth century, the British had developed such a strong habit that they established the first tea plantations in their colonies of India and Sri Lanka. The colonists had such an important influence on the teas of South Asia that I call them British Legacy Teas. I provide a more detailed history of tea in an appendix (page 205), since the history of tea is not as important to our purposes here as the tastes.

Within each chapter and throughout the book itself, I have arranged the teas as I would structure a traditional tasting. To prevent your taste buds from becoming overwhelmed, I always begin with the lightest, subtlest teas and end with the darkest and most intense. Whenever possible, I suggest that you taste the teas in each chapter all at once, in the order presented. That way you can compare them with one another and take in the entire range of flavors possible within each category. If you can dedicate an afternoon to tasting all the Chinese green teas in succession, come dinnertime you will know the full spectrum of flavors and aromas in Chinese green teas. That said, you should also feel free to dip into the book at your whim, learning in greater depth about your favorites, one or two at a time. Contrast is a great teacher; to best cultivate your palate for tea, taste at least two at once whenever possible. For further comparison, I have provided some tasting "menus" in an appendix (page 187).

I also offer a list of reliable tea sources whom I trust (page 211). Since these teas are some of the best in the world, you want to be sure to buy them from suppliers who know what they are doing. Some of the teas are expensive, but these shops often sell them in small packages of just an ounce or two. Just one note of caution: Unlike wine, tea does not come in vintages, though it changes from year to year. The teas I have selected for this book were at their peak when I tasted them, but over time they may not taste exactly the same to you as they did to me. As much as possible, I have chosen teas whose quality I expect to endure. But next year's Singbulli First Flush Darjeeling crop may simply be not as good as this year's, in spite of that garden's best efforts. Since you will be buying your tea at a different time, you may find that my tasting notes differ from yours. Ideally, my notes will still serve as a useful guide. However, another aim of this book is to give you the skills and confidence to disagree with me. After all, I am writing about matters of taste.

I will ask you to try a few odd rituals you may never have considered when making your usual cup. I will insist you set aside teabags and try a teapot and loose leaves. I will urge you to use a thermometer to check the water temperature before you brew. I suggest you use filtered water, not water straight from the tap. Once the tea is poured off, I will insist you jam your nose into the teapot to see how many aromas you can smell.

I have only one hard and fast rule, for myself as well as for you: Have fun. I learned this rule from the renowned German tea broker who first taught me how to taste tea like a professional. Bernd Wulf started working in the tea export business in Hamburg during the years after World War II (as you will read in the chapter on Darjeelings, in the 1960s and 1970s he helped radically transform First Flush Darjeeling black teas). In the late 1980s, Wulf founded his own prestigious tea exporting company, HamburgerTeeHandel (HTH). When his son Marcus joined HTH in the early 1990s, Marcus persuaded his father to sell some of their exquisite teas to our small American company.

On my first trip to Hamburg, Bernd showed me the traditional British way to taste teas, which I will teach you in this book's opening chapter. Bernd's most important lesson was to notice my own mood as I slurped and sipped. "Only buy teas that make you smile," he said. He paid close attention to how a tea made him feel as he tasted it. As he swirled the tea in his mouth, if his mouth fell into a frown, he would let someone else have that tea. If he found himself breaking into a grin, he would buy it. His rule has proven to be a profitable business principle for both our companies. It's that simple: A well-made tea makes you happy.

Tea should always be a pleasure. This master class is not being offered as a source of fresh reasons to feel inadequate. The joy of a cultivated tea palate is the ability to savor a beverage we too often take for granted. By no means bring out a water thermometer while rushing to get down your morning cup—get your day started first. Give yourself a tea lesson at a quieter moment, perhaps when your loved ones are at the zoo, not turning your home into one. And taste with a friend. Even though I've worked in tea for two decades, I always evaluate teas with a colleague.

On the road, I often travel with Marcus to tea farms and factories, where he and I taste together. Today, his family firm supplies us with 80 percent of our teas (you'll read about some of these trips in a few of the tea lessons as well). At my factory in Connecticut, I have a full-time co-taster, Elvira Cardenas, who has worked with me for nearly the last decade. Elvira is proof positive that connoisseurship is well within reach. She comes from Colombia, a country famous for its coffee. She started at Harney & Sons as a tea sorter just as I did, putting the teas into boxes and labeling them. Despite her initial bias for that harsher caffeine source, Elvira quickly rose through the ranks. Simply by paying close attention, she acquired an astonishing aptitude for discerning teas. Today, I rely on her judgment. I watch her mood as we taste together. Studies show we can quickly learn to discern flavors. The main focus of this book is to learn the tastes of tea. And that, dear tea lover, is pure joy.

HOW TO USE THIS BOOK

A Guide to Tasting Teas

The best thing you can do to taste these teas is to put yourself at ease. The art of tasting is the art of association. The only trick to identifying flavors and building your palate is to compare the teas with other foods you already know. Does the tea taste like spinach? leeks? roasted nuts? You have eaten a lifetime of foods, so you already have the necessary archive ready for retrieval.

Before you brew your first cup, imagine yourself on a leisurely stroll through the aisles of your favorite market. Get comfortable. Remind yourself of that important kindergarten lesson: There are no wrong answers. Old tea tasters have a favorite saying: "From ten tea tasters will come eleven opinions." Do whatever you need to do to relax, so that you can draw from the fullest spectrum of flavors and aromas you already know. The more at ease you are, the more you can take in about the tea.

To make it even easier, I've broken down tea tasting to five simple steps: (1) examining the dry leaves; (2) brewing the leaves at the proper time and temperature; (3) looking at the tea; (4) smelling the tea; and, only at the very end, (5) tasting the tea. In the chapters that follow, a tasting chart will introduce each new tea variety and guide you through each of the five steps.

1. EXAMINING THE DRY LEAVES

Tea leaves hold important clues to the quality of the eventual brew. The first step to tasting tea is to ensure you are brewing the right kind. Many of these teas are so rare that they are not always sold as the same grade. In each tasting chart I have provided a description of the appearance of the leaves; if yours look dramatically different, your tea may not be as good.

The leaves should look consistent with one another, as though they came from the same plant. Poorly made tea can have an odd mixture of shapes, from shoddy manufacturing or, worse, fraud, blending leaves from a variety of plants. Cheaply harvested tea will also contain bits of stalk. With the exception of Hojicha (page 66), an all-stalk tea, the best teas contain leaves only.

Next, examine the leaf size. If the chart says the leaves should be about one inch long but your tea leaves average a quarter of an inch or less, you have, unfortunately, bought an inferior tea. Lots of small particles will translate to a brisk, blunt taste. Similarly, some tea makers incorporate longer, older leaves when the finest versions include only the youngest and smallest.

Finally, check the dried leaves' aroma. The dry leaves offer a quick preview of the tea's taste. Breathe on the leaves through your mouth, as though you were clouding up a glass pane. The moisture will briefly trigger the release of the tea's aromas. Immediately inhale the moist breath through your nose. If the tea is stale, the aromas may seem subdued. Most good teas begin to go stale after six months and should not be drunk after two years.

Once you are confident your tea is good and fresh, measure it out. While water temperature and brewing times vary for each tea, the ratio of tea to water is constant: For 8 ounces of water, measure out 1 rounded teaspoon, or .079 ounces (2.2 grams).

❋ 2. BREWING THE LEAVES ❋

Potware

There is a world of potware to choose from, as wide as the world of tea. The selection can be overwhelming but doesn't have to be. Professional tasters brew tea in small lidded ceramic cups modeled on the Chinese *gaiwan* cup. Resembling demitasse cups, the vessels are ideal for smelling the drained leaves. Their vertical sides release the steam without condensing it, as a round pot might. The lids also help keep the steam contained. Professional cups are not necessary; any pot is fine. I prefer ceramic pots out of tradition; the Chinese and Japanese also favor pots of earthenware and iron; glass pots are increasingly popular to brew "art teas" whose leaves change shape in the hot water. Since you will smell the leaves in the pot, I suggest you use a ceramic or glass pot. The aromas of an earthenware or iron pot can interfere with the tea.

Cup

In order to judge the color of the tea, or the "liquor," it is important to use a white-lined ceramic cup. After brewing, professional tasters pour the tea into shallow, wide cups shaped like small cereal or café au lait bowls: The shallow spherical design helps expose the liquor to the light. Any white-lined cup will do.

Spoon

If you taste with a friend, you may both prefer to use a Chinese-style wide soup spoon to sample the tea instead of sipping directly from the cup. Although this is a common practice in professional settings involving many tasters, in a private tasting a spoon is entirely optional.

Water

There's a favorite saying in the tea world: "Water is the mother of tea." Before you start your teakettle, know that the chlorine and other chemicals in ordinary tap water will unfavorably affect the taste of these teas. Always use filtered water when tasting teas, unless you are fortunate enough to live near a spring; spring water is ideal.

Brewing Temperature

Different teas require different temperatures to fully release their flavors; generally speaking, the darker the tea, the hotter the water needed. Water boils at 212 degrees Fahrenheit, but that heat will scorch white and green teas. Their more delicate flavors best emerge between 160 and 190 degrees Fahrenheit. Most of the finest black teas taste best brewed at only 205 degrees Fahrenheit or so. You can buy electric water-dispensing pots, machines that heat water to precise temperatures. These machines are not necessary; just insert an instant-read thermometer into the spout of your kettle to gauge your water temperature before pouring the water over the leaves. Sometimes I give a range rather than a precise temperature; as with brewing time (see below), the exact temperature can vary with each batch of tea. Experiment to see what works best.

Brewing Time

Different teas brew best for different lengths of time; the darker the tea, the longer the brewing time. My brewing times are offered as guidelines only, as every tea is different: My box of Lung Ching may need three minutes, while yours may need only two. Observing both the tea liquor and body will help you gauge whether you have brewed your tea for the correct amount of time.

3. LOOKING AT THE TEA

The technical term for brewed tea is "liquor." Knowing the ideal color of the liquor can also help you assess whether you've brewed the tea correctly. If you pour off something that looks darker or lighter than the color described in the tasting charts, you may have over- or underbrewed it. No matter—teas are so variable, even professional tasters often brew them imperfectly at first. Just start over, noting your adjustments for future tastings.

4. SMELLING THE TEA

Your nose is far more sensitive than your mouth when it comes to detecting flavor. Roughly speaking, your mouth can detect only four tastes: sweet, sour, bitter, and salty. Some say there are five, if you count the mouth-filling quality the Japanese call "*umami*." Everything else—floral, fruity, piney, briny—we register through our noses. Wine tasters smell the wine itself before drinking, swirling the liquid in the glass to release the volatile aromatic compounds. Tea tasters don't smell the tea, they smell the brewed tea leaves.

After draining the leaves, give them a minute to cool off. The very first smells will be only water, as the vaporizing rate of water is faster than that of the aromatic compounds in the leaves. After any danger of steam burns has passed, bury

13

your nose in the pot. Don't hold back—the first sign of a good tea taster is a few wet tea leaves stuck to the nose.

Breathe in through the nose and inhale deeply. Take several breaths if you need to in order to isolate and identify the scents. The aromas will begin to dissipate, but if you close the pot again, they will regather beneath the lid as they rise. Wait a few minutes, then smell again. This is where envisioning your favorite market or garden can really help. Do you smell gardenias in that oolong? honeysuckle in the white? papaya or some other tropical fruit in the Darjeeling? The aromas I provide in the tasting charts are ones I detected, but you may well find others. Make a note of them and see whether they come out in the flavors when you sip the tea later. Sometimes the aromas will match the tastes, but this is a quality prized in single-malt Scotches, not much in teas. Sometimes the aromas simply add another, complementary dimension to what is already a great-tasting tea.

5. TASTING THE TEA

Finally, take a sip. Professional tea tasters don't just drink the tea, they slurp it the way one might slurp hot soup. The point is not to cool the tea, but to aerate it, to allow more of the aromas to drift up to the olfactory region—the nose—to smell the tea as well as to taste it. If you find the tea is too hot, wait a few minutes more. The tea should be warm but not scalding.

Pull sharply on the tea, inhaling quickly through your mouth to run it between your lips and teeth. Don't be afraid to slurp really loudly; on tea-buying trips in Asia, I've impressed tea brokers there that I slurp as noisily as they do, if not more so. It's not a competition; they just don't expect Westerners to know how to do this. Once you have the aerated tea in your mouth, swish it around with your tongue and cheeks to give every last taste bud a chance to try it out.

Body

Now assess the weight of the tea: Does it feel thin like water or thick like cream? "Body" refers to a tea's heft or weight, how much substance or texture it has. White teas and Chinese green teas are very light, feeling almost like water. Thicker Japanese green teas often feel brothy, a little like chicken soup with their greater heft. Some oolongs are actually called "creamy" for the way they coat your mouth like heavy cream. Black teas have a different kind of heft: Their body is often described as brisk or astringent, for the way they dry up the mouth.

A tea's body is also among the best indicators of brew strength. While a poorly brewed tea will still release plenty of aromas, its body will suffer. Does the tea feel thin or wan? Even the lightest teas should have a little texture; a thin tea probably needs more time to brew and may also need a pinch more dry leaves. Alternatively, does it taste bitter and make your mouth pucker? Then the tea may be overbrewed. With many British Legacy Teas, this strength is normal, but the bulk of the teas in this book should taste mellow, rounded, and balanced.

Flavors

Once you have established the tea's aromas and body, at long last you can begin to tease out its flavors. Using the chart as a point of departure, ask yourself what else the tea tastes like: spinach? mangoes? Keep tasting: Like great wines, the teas will change their flavors the longer you hold them in your mouth. The flavors will also evolve as the tea cools and, in some instances, as with puerhs and oolongs, as you rebrew the leaves. You may find more flavors than the ones I have included in the tea charts; note them down. After you've swallowed the tea, see how long you can continue to taste it. The final mark of a great tea is how long its flavor endures in the mouth after you've swallowed. This endurance is called a tea's "finish," or "aftertaste," and for some teas it can last as long as ten to fifteen minutes.

That's all there is to it. In many entries, I have augmented these charts with background information to deepen your knowledge of the teas. For more on the chemistry and history, I strongly encourage you to consult the appendixes. All you really need to do to become a tea connoisseur is to taste a lot of tea. Now you know how. Let's go taste the finest teas the world has to offer.

WHITE TEAS

1. *Yin Zhen*

2. *Bai Mei*

3. *Ceylon Silver Tips*

4. *Bai Mu Dan*

Something of a tabula rasa of the tea world, white teas offer an ideal starting point for an aspiring tea connoisseur. Barely processed, light, and refined, they present one of the purest expressions of the tea plant. They are not exactly white—the tea buds grow to a bright green color, fade to silver, and brew to a pale yellow. The liquor yields not only the lightest color, but also the leanest body of all teas, a delicate juxtaposition to the creaminess of oolongs and the brisk pucker of British Legacy Teas. Their aromas and flavors are wonderfully subtle, requiring careful attention. Look for gentle sweet notes ranging from honeysuckle to light maple sap, citrus fruit flavors like orange and lemon, and wisps of floral aromas, evoking jasmine and rose.

What gives white tea these ethereal qualities? The bud. Where green and black teas draw their more robust qualities from mature leaves, white teas consist

CHINA • TAIWAN

China/Taiwan Boundary
International Boundary
Province-level Boundary
River

★ National Capital
⊙ Province-level Capital
● City or Town
Mountain Range

© 2008 Meighan Cavanaugh

China

BEIJING

ANHUI
Tai Hu
HUANGSHAN
HANGZHOU
ZHEJIANG
Yangtze River
Dongting Hu
WUYI SHAN
FU'AN
PANYANG
HUNAN
XIPING
FUJIAN
FENGHUANG
GUANGDONG
YUNNAN
HONG KONG

East China Sea

PING LING

ALI SHAN

Taiwan

N

of incipient leaves called "buds," or "tips." If left unplucked, within a week to ten days this bud would unfurl into a beautiful leaf. White tea buds are plucked and "withered," or "air-dried." During the drying, they turn from light green to iridescent silver as the immature chlorophyll within them dies off. While the evergreen tea plant sprouts these buds year-round, the tips hold particularly delicious flavors in the springtime, when the plant sends out a flush of nutrients it has stored over the cool winter.

To help the buds mature into leaves, the plants furnish them with an extra shot of glucose, a sugar boost that makes the buds much sweeter than a mature leaf. To protect the buds from sun and bugs, the plants also provide them with a downy soft coating of tiny hairs called "tricomes." These tricomes give the buds a soft fuzziness like pussy willows and can sometimes coat dry tea leaves in a fine pale dust. The downy fur helps limit water loss and may also deter hungry bugs from gaining access to the nutrients within. To further deter predators, buds also contain extra caffeine and polyphenols, a natural sunblock and bug repellent. White teas are therefore slightly more caffeinated than green and black teas. Their greater proportion of polyphenols may also make them healthier, since polyphenols act as antioxidants in humans. While we can hope that antioxidants help prevent cancer and heart disease, the science remains inconclusive.

Consisting only of buds, white teas are the simplest yet also among the most complex. Their sizable tips are a product of centuries of selective propagation. Buds play an important role in many green and black teas; harvested along with mature leaves, they give those teas refined sweetness and a softer body. White teas therefore provide a chance to sample an important component of tea, barely adulterated.

White teas have recently become so popular that tea makers have begun making them all over the world, most recently in Kenya. For now, however, the very best come from Fujian province in China and increasingly from Sri Lanka in South Asia. The coastal province of Fujian has played a crucial role in the evolution of tea. Both oolongs and black teas likely first emerged here. The famous smoky black tea Lapsang Souchong comes from the province's Wuyi Mountains. Tea makers here have produced white teas in earnest only within the last two hundred years. When the British stopped buying tea from China in favor of their own gardens in India, the British demand for Fujian teas diminished. Tea makers responded with a concerted effort to develop other specialty teas.

We begin with Fujian's Yin Zhen, or "Silver Needles." Its perfect downy buds, round body, and pale, slightly vegetal sweetness make it arguably the finest white tea in the world. Next we will try Bai Mei, a charming tea from China's more central Hunan province, whose buds are sewn together to resemble plum blossoms. Then we will sample Ceylon Silver Tips, a tea from the emerging white tea source Sri Lanka and a challenger to Yin Zhen's throne. Though one of the newest white teas, Ceylon Silver Tips has a compelling charm to it. We close with Bai Mu Dan, another Chinese white whose mix of buds and leaves nearly qualifies it as a green tea. Bai Mu Dan will lead us elegantly into the ensuing chapter on Chinese green teas.

These teas are all so delicate, they brew best at a low temperature and for a short period: around 175 degrees Fahrenheit and for only two to three minutes. The water changes color so imperceptibly, I suggest you use my flavor guides as well as the liquor colors to judge whether the teas have brewed enough.

YIN ZHEN
Silver Needles

BREWING TEMPERATURE	175°F.
BREWING TIME	2–3 minutes.
DRY LEAVES	Yin Zhen has no leaves, only slender, inch-long dried buds. Also called tips or silver needles, the buds are so fuzzy with tricomes, they look like slender pussy willows.
LIQUOR	A very pale yellow green, sometimes with a rose cast to it.
AROMAS	Smelling of wet, sweet hay, with a glaze of sugar, like cotton candy. Light floral high notes of honeysuckle and jasmine.
BODY	Fuller relative to other white teas, but still quite thin.
FLAVORS	Yin Zhen can sometimes begin tasting only of water. But it quickly blooms in the mouth to show a light sugar sweetness, dulled with gentle vegetal flavors of steamed bok choy. Some versions also have faint "heat" notes, like toasted white bread.

Yin Zhen is widely considered the best white tea in the world. Although it is expensive, it merits its price. It comes from a beautiful corner of Fujian province whose hills and valleys are carpeted with gorgeous tea gardens. The best Yin Zhen comes from the coastal counties of Fuding and neighboring Zheng He, whose mountains are steep but not high. Yin Zhen's silver tips grow on the *Da Bai* ("big white") tea tree, whose name aptly describes the plant's large buds. The *Da Bai* plant forms fat buds, thickly coated with down. The plants need time to create these big buds, so the Yin Zhen harvest starts later than in adjacent green tea areas.

The buds are painstakingly plucked by hand. In the spring, in the mornings after the dew has dried, the hills are dotted with harvesters. Typical of the variation within many Chinese teas, every Yin Zhen maker makes this tea a little differently. Some tea makers dry the buds on tarps in the sun, others dry them on wooden slats in the shade, and still others lay them out on racks in temperature-controlled rooms. A few Yin Zhen makers lightly fire the teas after drying them, giving their teas the faint heat flavors of lightly toasted white bread.

Yin Zhen is just as charming for the way it brews. It is worth steeping Yin Zhen in a glass vessel to watch this. Instead of pouring the water over the buds, scatter the buds over the surface of the water. Sometimes the buds will fall right to the bottom, but in the best of times they will float a few moments on the surface, then tip their noses to hang vertically in the water. There they will sway gently, before falling to the bottom of the glass. As they unleash a pale green liquor, the buds themselves will slowly turn a dark sage green.

BAI MEI

White Eyebrow

BREWING TEMPERATURE	175°F.
BREWING TIME	2–3 minutes.
DRY LEAVES	Made entirely of silver-green tips hand-sewn to form six-petaled flowers. Each tip is ½ inch long. The small florettes remind the Chinese of plum blossoms.
LIQUOR	Pale yellow.
AROMAS	Though still very light, Bai Mei is more assertive and more vegetal than Yin Zhen. It smells of the faint sweetness of roasted leeks, shifting to honey after a few minutes.
BODY	Fuller and rounder than Yin Zhen, but still very light.
FLAVORS	Soft and subtle, Bai Mei gently suffuses the mouth with the sweet vegetal flavors of roasted leeks, along with the floral qualities of lily of the valley along the edges.

This charming tea provides an engaging example of the slightly more assertive, more vegetal flavors of white teas from the center of China. Bai Mei also captures the beauty of Chinese art teas, teas whose leaves are manipulated to form charming shapes. Bai Mei comes from China's central Hunan province, where tea is an ancient art form. White tea has been made there—some would say perfected there—for centuries. The region produced small amounts of white teas during the Qing dynasty, but it was only in the late 1800s that white teas emerged from the area in significant amounts.

Bai Mei means "White Eyebrow," which is a little what the large tips look like when they are loose. Bai Mei is handmade by skilled workers, usually women, who sew six long buds together with string, then gently flatten them out to shape the connected buds into flowers resembling plum blossoms. When submerged in hot water, the flowers plump up to release a delicate sweet brew with the faintly sappy flavors of a classic, refined white tea.

CEYLON SILVER TIPS

BREWING TEMPERATURE	175°F.
BREWING TIME	2–3 minutes.
DRY LEAVES	No leaves, only slender, slightly curved silver buds just over 1 inch long. With less of the downy tricomes than other white teas, Ceylon Silver Tips look more like tiny skewers than pussy willows.
LIQUOR	Pale yellow.
AROMAS	The very gentlest citrus-spice suggestion of oranges stuck with cloves; subtly sweet.
BODY	Medium light; halfway between the gossamer Yin Zhen and the rounder Bai Mei.
FLAVORS	Hints of oranges and cloves, but also green grapes, honeycrisp apples, and—in the finish—a little jasmine.

Ceylon Silver Tips is one of the few exquisite white teas now available outside China. Where Chinese white teas have a faint vegetal undertone, Ceylon Silver Tips is nearly all fruit, flowers, and sweetness. As its name suggests, this tea comes from Sri Lanka, formerly known as Ceylon. An island south of India, Sri Lanka produces many wonderful black teas (see "Ceylon Black Teas," page 153).

In the tiny world of white tea production, Sri Lanka has more recently become the second largest white tea producer after China.

Ceylon Silver Tips has appeared only within the last few decades. It comes from an area about halfway up the Central Highlands, the high mountain range that divides the tropical island. Unlike the large operations in Fujian province that produce Bai Mu Dan (page 27), Ceylon white teas come from small gardens with wonderful names like Oodoowerre and Meddecombra. Only some of the plants yield the necessarily large tip. As a result, tea is produced in such small quantities that buying more than a dozen boxes requires significant haggling. The tea's subtle citrus fruit and spice flavors make the effort worthwhile.

BAI MU DAN

White Peony

BREWING TEMPERATURE	175°F.
BREWING TIME	2–3 minutes.
DRY LEAVES	A mix of silver-green 1-inch-long tips and forest green leaves. The better the tea, the more tips—and the greener the leaves. Lesser varieties have large brown leaves (and a duller, harsher flavor).
LIQUOR	Yellow green; the darkest of all whites.
AROMAS	Light vegetal aromas glazed with sugar, like the sweet-charred quality of roasted leeks.
BODY	Medium light, though full-bodied for a white tea.
FLAVORS	The finest fill the mouth with the light, sweet vegetal flavor of steamed yellow squash. Those versions that have been dried in ovens or over charcoal also have the faint "heat" taste of toasted walnuts.

Among the most popular and easy to find of the white teas, Bai Mu Dan also bridges the gap between white teas and green with its mixture of tips and whole tea leaves and resulting mild vegetal flavors. A relative of Yin Zhen (page 21), Bai Mu Dan comes from the same cultivar. Unlike any other white tea in this chapter, Bai Mu Dan also includes some mature tea leaves. The finest have the highest ratio of buds to leaves. Lower-grade Bai Mu Dan is easy to spot with its large, green-brown leaves, dark and gangly from growing too long on the plant. The best Bai Mu Dan is harvested in late April and the first half of May. Bai Mu Dan is air-dried, making its vegetal flavors milder than green teas', veering to yellow squash rather than the more robust flavors of artichokes or spinach. Sometimes the tea is finished over a coal fire or in an oven, which gives the tea a faint roasted flavor.

Bai Mu Dan was developed in the early twentieth century in northern Fujian province. Over the ensuing decades, the production area migrated to the coastal region around the big Fujian province port city of Fuding. Unlike the previous three teas, which are rarer, Bai Mu Dan is produced in quantities large enough to fill many shipping containers every spring. The tea's international popularity is understandable. It bridges the best of two worlds, offering the savory, vegetal satisfaction of a green tea along with the sweetness and subtlety of a great white.

CHINESE GREEN TEAS

ou've mastered the flavors of white teas made just with buds; now with Chinese green teas you get your first experience of mature tea leaves that have been not merely air-dried, but cooked to preserve their color and enhance their flavor. While milder than most black teas, green teas are considerably more assertive than whites, with a fuller, rounder body, a darker liquor, and delicious vegetal flavors.

Although green teas now grow all over the world, the finest come from China and Japan. I begin with China's in small part because they have a much deeper history: China has been producing tea for at least the last five thousand years, while the Japanese have made tea in earnest for just the last five hundred. Far more significant for your palate, however, I start with Chinese greens because they are lighter and less intense. Sharing some of the sweetness of white teas, they make for a more natural choice to follow whites in our tasting progression. Compared with the darker, more mouth-filling Japanese green teas, Chinese greens have the gentler vegetal flavors of steamed leeks, green beans, or bok choy. And where Japanese greens have no sugariness, Chinese greens have charming sweet notes of cooked carrots, jasmine, and sometimes a subtle hint of honey.

Much of this sweetness begins in the fields, stemming from the same component in white tea: the bud. The best Chinese green teas are hand-harvested in the spring from "leafsets," consisting of a bud and its two adjacent leaves. Plucked over a tiny window of just ten to fourteen days in late March or early April, these springtime leafsets hold more sugars and other flavor compounds than leaves at any other time of year. As the temperature rises and the plant emerges from winter dormancy, the roots send out stored glucose and other flavor compounds to the buds to restart growth. Spring teas may also have more antioxidants, as the plant sends out extra polyphenols to protect the leaves from bugs. In China, these springtime teas are sometimes called Qing Ming teas, since their harvest begins around the same time as China's Qing Ming spring festival.

The light flavors of Chinese greens emerge only after the leaves have been plucked and then fixed. When tea makers "fix" green teas, they preserve the chlorophyll by quickly heating the leaves after harvest. The heat destroys the enzyme that would otherwise turn the leaves brown. The same enzyme browns an apple or potato when the flesh is exposed to the air; just as cooking apples or potatoes preserves their white color, fixing tea keeps it green.

While the Japanese fix their teas by steaming them, Chinese tea makers use a panoply of methods, each with their own flavors. Legend tells us the first tea was blanched when a fresh leaf fell by chance into a bowl of hot water. Tea makers later steamed teas—it was from the Chinese that the Japanese learned the technique in the ninth century—but then began fixing the leaves in hot woks. Today, some tea makers in China also fix teas in bamboo cylinders or ovens with blasts of hot air.

Woks and ovens affect Chinese green teas in two ways: They sweeten the leaves further by searing them, and they fix the leaves more slowly, allowing them to develop a wider range of aromatic compounds. The searing occurs because woks and ovens get much hotter than boiling water. Boiling water peaks at 212 degrees Fahrenheit, but an oven ranges from 300 to 400 degrees Fahrenheit, and a wok can get as hot as 1,200 degrees Fahrenheit. This much higher heat causes what chemists call "the Maillard reaction," the creation within the leaves of compounds called "glucosides." These glucose-derived compounds give the leaves pleasant toasted, sometimes nutty, sugared notes much as a skillet gives a pancake. The sweetness is very subtle; those who like their tea with two teaspoonfuls of table sugar may still want to add something extra. But compared with the decidedly unsugared, darker, and more vegetal Japanese green teas, Chinese green teas have a distinctly honeyed edge.

Wok and oven fixing also makes Chinese greens slightly more aromatic, with slightly sweeter scents than Japanese greens. All teas begin to develop their aromas as soon as they are plucked. Cut off from their nutrient source, the stressed leaves send warnings in the form of aromatic compounds to alert the rest of the plant of an attack. Among the first aromas to emerge are scents of lemon and fresh-cut grass. In the case of oolongs, these warnings change to jasmine and gardenia as tea makers "wither" the leaves, letting them desiccate slowly over a period of hours. Chinese and Japanese green tea leaves wither over just the short trip from the field to the factory. Chinese green teas wither a little longer than Japanese green teas because they are fixed more gradually—since wok fixing takes much more time than steaming. If you've ever stir-fried broccoli as opposed to blanching it, you know the difference: Stirring the raw vegetable over even a very hot pan cooks it more slowly than boiling-hot water will. That added time means the plant can continue to send out its scented distress signals. A comparison of the aromas in a Japanese Sencha and a Chinese wok-fired green tea shows that the Sencha has more lemony "linalools," while the wok-fired tea has more carroty "beta ionones" and "neriols," floral aromas more common to oolongs, which wither for a much longer period. (It's important to note, however, that neither Japanese nor Chinese green teas have anywhere near the concentration of aromas in oolongs or even black teas.)

Moving in order of lightest and sweetest to darkest and most intense, we'll start with Pan Long Ying Hao, the green tea with the largest bud, most closely resembling a white tea in its sweetness and pale hue. We'll taste progressively more vegetal greens, including China's famous Lung Ching, considered a standard for its flavors of honey, toasted nuts, and steamed green vegetables. Then we'll try Dragon Pearl, a green tea perfumed with jasmine blossoms. We'll end with Gunpowder, perhaps the darkest green tea available in China or Japan, wok-fired to give it a rich, roasted, smoky flavor.

Pay close attention to the leaves in this chapter: From Lung Ching's slender grasshopper wings, to Bi Lo Chun's coiled snail shells, to Taiping HouKui's spindly, chartreuse filaments resembling shards of spinach linguine, you won't find this variety of shapes anywhere else. Chinese tea makers sometimes also manipulate the buds to draw out their fuzzy down, so much so that some teas like Bi Lo Chun are coated in fuzzy golden dust. No matter their ultimate shape, the leaves often remain in their original harvested trio: tidy leafsets of two leaves and a bud, joined at the stem. It's well worth drawing out the leafsets after brewing these teas to see for yourself.

Up until even five years ago, few of these teas made it to the West. Most are made for local markets and in tiny quantities. The more Westerners have learned about fine teas and gained a willingness to pay for them, the more these teas have made their way across the oceans. The health benefits of green tea in particular have helped boost their popularity; like white teas, green teas have plenty of antioxidants (polyphenols), which have been shown to help fight chronic illness. In black teas, some of these polyphenols degrade into other compounds—indeed, into the very chemicals that turn black tea brown. Hence green teas have more antioxidants than black teas.

Chinese green teas can be brewed fairly consistently. The filtered water or spring water should be around 175 degrees Fahrenheit, so as not to scorch the delicate tea. It is best not to rinse the teapot with hot water, as this would raise the brewing temperature too high. Brewing time is from two to three minutes; these teas yield their flavors much more quickly than black teas do.

PAN LONG YING HAO

Dragon Silver Hair

BREWING TEMPERATURE	175°F.
BREWING TIME	2–3 minutes.
DRY LEAVES	Gently twisted small, whole leaves ranging from dark sage green to chartreuse, along with fuzzy white tips, loosely coiled like fibrous, fraying ropes.
LIQUOR	Pale yellow green.
AROMAS	The sweetness of braised spring leeks with hints of lightly sweetened cocoa.
BODY	Light.
FLAVORS	Even, smooth, and confident. Lightly sweetened cocoa in the top notes, sweet braised leeks in the base, and a long-lasting honeyed finish with the faintest hint of gardenia.

We start with Pan Long Ying Hao because it is the "whitest" of the green teas in this chapter. It most resembles a white tea with its large buds, fuzzy tips that give the tea light, sweet flavors of steamed spring leeks.

The coastal Chinese province of Zhejiang is famous for its green teas, particularly Gunpowder and Lung Ching. As many as fifty other teas are made in the province's hinterlands. An amazing bounty, but nearly impossible to obtain, as most are grown for such a confined local market. Pan Long Ying Hao is one exception, a local tea invented for local drinkers perhaps thirty years ago, but now available in the West.

Pan Long Ying Hao is such an obscure tea, it is difficult to learn how it is made. It likely gets its tip from a particular cultivar bred for large, downy sprouts. Given its lightly sweet, roasted flavors, it is probably fixed in a hot wok. The leaves are so loosely shaped, they must be rolled only very delicately. The rolling also teases out the down in the buds, to make the tips soft like pussy willows. The final drying presumably creates the tea's lovely cocoa notes. This is a calming tea, whose flavors evolve in the mouth like a slowly moving stream.

JIN SHAN
Jin Mountain

BREWING TEMPERATURE	175°F.
BREWING TIME	2–3 minutes.
DRY LEAVES	Silvery tips and spindly stiff leaves twisted like barbed wire, about 1 inch long and sage green, with flecks of forest green and white down.
LIQUOR	Golden yellow.
AROMAS	A compelling mixture of floral, citrus, and vegetal aromas: orange blossoms and grapefruit as well as steamed green beans.
BODY	Light, somewhat astringent.
FLAVORS	All but singing out with a mouth-filling flavor of sweet roasted artichokes, Jin Shan also has a lemony finish and an engaging tinge of roasted marshmallow from its coal firing.

Full of personality, Jin Shan brings us closer to characteristic Chinese green teas with its citrusy, vegetal, and roasted flavors. The tea has smaller white tips than Pan Long Ying Hao and is more heavily fired. As a result, it offers a more assertive, classic green tea flavor.

Jin Shan is both a tea and an ancient tea-growing region. The bushes thrive in the cool mountains that separate Zhejiang from Anhui province. Surrounded by stately pine and bamboo forests, like many of China's earliest tea-growing regions, Jin Shan is located just outside a large Buddhist monastery. The monks here developed the tea for their own consumption, for tribute to the emperor, and for sale to support the monastery. Monks in Jin Shan may well have also played a tremendous role in tea history, introducing Japan to green tea when in the ninth century they gave Jin Shan tea to monks visiting from that smaller island. Recent genetic tests have shown that Japanese green teas derive from the teas grown in this region.

Jin Shan monks also taught local farmers their methods, and this time-refined knowledge was passed down through the centuries—until the twentieth century, when the Communist regime shut down these religious institutions. Happily, the monastery has recently been rebuilt, and tea producers are expanding and modernizing both the tea gardens and their small tea factory.

To give this tea its characteristic light, sweet flavors, Jin Shan producers expose the leaves to as little heat as possible. First they fix the leaves with a quick blast of hot air. To give the leaves their spindly, twisted shape, they manipulate the wilted leaves with their hands in a hot wok, but only very briefly to keep the tea from taking on excessive roasted flavors. Finally, they fire the tea for a short time in a *poey long*, a bamboo cylinder unique to China. Fired so quickly, the tea takes on just a hint of charcoal flavors, evocative of crisp roasted marshmallows.

BI LO CHUN

Spring Snail Shell

BREWING TEMPERATURE	175°F.
BREWING TIME	2–3 minutes.
DRY LEAVES	A mixture of dark green, almost bluish gray, spiraled, wiry filaments coated in fuzzy yellow down. The filaments are so fine, this tea stales quickly and should be consumed within 6 months.
LIQUOR	Pale green, slightly cloudy from the down.
AROMAS	Light and sweet, with the roasted sweetness of brown sugar and a vegetal base note of steamed green beans. Fainter citrusy, floral scents of orange blossoms.
BODY	Light, though more astringent than Jin Shan. It dries out the mouth a little.
FLAVORS	The faintest hint of jasmine is nearly overmatched by the roasted, vegetal flavor of grilled endive. In the finish, the vegetal flavors resolve back to the floral tinge of jasmine and orange blossoms.

Tightly wound like tiny snail shells, the leaves of Bi Lo Chun unfurl into tidy leafsets of two leaves and a bud when they're brewed, yielding cloudy, pale green liquor full of sparkle. Fixed and fired over raging hot woks, Bi Lo Chun is not quite as classically vegetal as Lung Ching (page 40). Instead, the tea offers more pronounced roasted vegetal flavors of grilled endive, with that vegetable's engaging, nearly bitter bite, along with charming floral and citrus flavors.

Unlike the relatively recent Pan Long Ying Hao or the obscure Jin Shan, Bi Lo Chun is a popular tea and an ancient one, enjoyed by emperors and mere mortals throughout China for several centuries. One of the most northern teas made in China, Bi Lo Chun comes from a tiny island called Dongting on the Tai Hu, or Tai Lake. The lake lies two hours north of the city of Hangzhou on the southern border of Jiangsu province. It is a lovely spot. Moisture off the lake moderates the otherwise cold and harsh climate, making tea cultivation possible. The island is also home to fruit orchards, and in an unusual arrangement, the tea bushes are interspersed among the trees. The tea is said to draw its aromas from the apricot and plum blossoms, but this claim is questionable. The tea does not taste much of flowers, and most of the trees bloom only after the Qing Ming spring festival, after Bi Lo Chun has been harvested. The fruit orchards do make for a lovely setting, though.

I visited Jiangsu province for the first time only recently, on a tea-buying trip with Marcus Wulf, a friend and my tea broker. We went at the tail end of Qing Ming season, in late April toward the end of the harvest. Through some surprising circumstances, we realized that the tea production is so small, most makers of Bi Lo Chun have to supplement their income with other work.

We started the trip in Hangzhou, a large metropolis that produces Lung Ching, another famous Chinese green tea. Though Hangzhou lies only two hours south of Dongting island, the two tea regions are worlds apart. Compared with the crowded, more southern city, Dongting island could not be more isolated or remote. We asked some Lung Ching brokers in Hangzhou if they could help us find our way there (they had sold Marcus Bi Lo Chun tea, so we assumed they knew the way). They happily agreed, but after several hours in their car meandering the empty back roads of Jiangsu province, we realized they had no idea where we were. We found a hotel that would take us for the night, figuring we'd find our way back to Hangzhou in the morning. Surprised to see Westerners, the hotel doorman asked us what we were doing there. Through our translator, I explained that we wanted to see Bi Lo Chun farms on Dongting island. He smiled and told us he owned one. He offered to take us there the next day.

The next morning, we pulled up to his operation. Though his was one of the larger factories, the facilities were still small and rudimentary. The tea making made for a mesmerizing sight: Workers fixed the freshly harvested leaves in big woks heated with pulsing coal fires. With their callused hands, the workers pushed the leaves against the hot metal in a sweeping motion that teased out the tip. At first, the tips grew big and fluffy. As the leaves curled up into their snail shell shape, the down spread out over the leaves in a fine golden dust.

Passing through the small factory to the gardens in back, I was astonished to see how much work is required to harvest the leafsets. In ordinary tea gardens, the bushes are arrayed in close and easily trimmable rows. Here harvesters had to wander through the orchards for long stretches from bush to bush, often stooping low to reach the branches. In the cold and damp, I could feel how the early spring temperatures slowed the growth of the leaves, concentrating their flavors.

To warm up we ducked into a cottage serving lunch. We dined on fish from the lake that had been poached in a lesser-grade tea, likely made from the same bushes. While we were given some of the tea to try when we first arrived, during lunch they gave us beer. The small island of Dongting can't be more than fifteen square miles. Bi Lo Chun is produced in such tiny quantities, harvested only one or two times for the whole year, the locals don't drink very much of it. Before my visit, I used to nag Marcus to secure more Bi Lo Chun for me. Now I'm grateful I can get the thirty-odd kilos a year that I do. Though it is one of China's most popular green teas, its tiny production keeps it rare and exceptional.

LUNG CHING
Dragon's Well

BREWING TEMPERATURE	175°F.
BREWING TIME	2–3 minutes.
DRY LEAVES	The stiff but silky-smooth, spearlike leaf is flat and narrow, about 1 inch long. Though it looks like a single flat needle, the unit actually comprises two leaves joined at a stem.
LIQUOR	Pale yellow.
AROMAS	Steamed bok choy and toasted walnuts, with top notes of sweet spring grass.
BODY	Medium light.
FLAVORS	The delicious meatiness of roasted eggplant, with similar steamed bok choy and toasted walnut flavors as in the aromas. Some vegetal sweetness of spring clover.

Lung Ching is to Chinese green teas what French Champagne is to sparkling white wines: the standard against which all others are measured. One of China's best and most well-known teas, Lung Ching comes fourth in this chapter because of its relative sweetness. With almost no tip, it has the classic Chinese green tea qualities of steamed bok choy and toasted nuts. The Lung Ching cultivar produces a tiny, almost undetectable bud. With far less of the sugariness that glazes the preceding teas, the tea fills the mouth with vegetal flavor. This is a confident, savory tea.

Though Xi Hu, or the West Lake, has been producing tea for centuries, Lung Ching became a tribute tea during the Qing dynasty. (Historically, emperors commanded favored teas as tributes. As in the case of Lung Ching, selection as a tribute tea meant financial success and enduring fame.) Lung Ching means "Dragon's Well," which refers to an old well halfway up a hill outside Hangzhou, in Zhejiang province, where the tea was originally grown.

Lung Ching still comes from the hills around the province's capital city. Today, Hangzhou is one of the best cities in the world for tea. Once the capital of the southern Song dynasty, in the twelfth and thirteenth centuries it became a hub for Arab and Persian traders at the heart of China's silk trade. Described by Marco Polo as one of the noblest cities in the world, Hangzhou remains one of China's most cultured and sophisticated cities, much of its life centered around the lovely tea made on the far side of its West Lake.

In a city of just over one million, more than seven hundred teahouses cater to every taste. The salons serve Lung Ching along with pastries and simple snacks such as oranges and pumpkin seeds. Many Chinese state officials have country homes along the beautiful West Lake. The Chinese government officially lionized this famous tea by establishing a National Tea Museum in Hangzhou. The city is also home to a tea research institute and a prominent agricultural university boasting one of China's best departments devoted to tea.

The demand for spring Lung Ching is so great that not all of the supply comes from the hills of Hangzhou. Prudence is required to secure the authentic spring leaves. True spring Lung Ching takes its light, slightly toasted flavor from being fixed and fired by hand in electrically heated woks. Expert tea makers press the leaves against the hot metal with their fingers. Through many deft motions, the workers flatten the leafsets of two leaves until they appear to be one flat, spear-like unit. This ancient method of fixing and firing the teas is performed in several stages, so the tea does not scorch but takes on the light toasted flavor of walnuts. The delicate, nutty result makes authentic Lung Ching well worth seeking out.

HUANGSHAN MAO FENG
Yellow Mountain Downy Tip

BREWING TEMPERATURE	175°F.
BREWING TIME	2–3 minutes.
DRY LEAVES	Small but plump leaves and buds, with a slight curve to them. The best of these pale yellow leaves show a fine sheen of down.
LIQUOR	Light green.
AROMAS	A vegetal base of steamed Napa cabbage, with the slight toasted notes of pecans.
BODY	Lighter than Lung Ching, but with a slight coating at the back of the mouth.
FLAVORS	The vegetal, almost starchy flavor of lima beans, along with the faint sweetness of carrots, evoking succotash but still lean and refreshing.

This subdued, mature tea has the starchy, vegetal flavor of lima beans with the faint sweetness of carrots. Its assertive vegetal character belies its delicate creation. Huangshan Mao Feng comes from a picturesque corner of the interior province of Anhui. The stunning Huangshan, or Yellow Mountains, are a UNESCO world heritage site and include peaks as high as four thousand feet. At that altitude, clouds regularly enshroud the area, providing a moist, cool climate ideal for tea. The plants grow in the lower elevations, closer to the main town of Tunxi. Huangshan Mao Feng is the finest green tea from this area, which also produces the less tender and less fragrant Huangshan Mao Jian later in the season. As I saw on a recent trip to the Yellow Mountains, everything about Huangshan Mao Feng tea is refined.

My broker, Marcus Wulf, and I started in Tunxi, looking for tea sources. We drove to an organic garden several hours outside the town. The mountain road could not have been more idyllic, twisting up the tree-lined mountains alongside a rushing stream. We found harvesters out in the mist gathering the tips and leaves. We could see our breath, the air was so cold.

Ordinarily, pickers toss fistfuls of tea into vast hampers strapped to their backsides. The leaves of the Huangshan Mao Feng are so small that these harvesters nestled the leafsets into holders no more than a few inches in diameter. Once their tiny baskets were full, the harvesters descended on foot to the nearby village, where the tea was processed. The mist was rolling in with the sunset; we were loath to leave such a pretty spot. But we were also anxious to watch the tea being made, so we followed them and strolled through town.

Most of the teas in this chapter are made entirely by hand; Huangshan is one of the few made almost entirely by machines. At the Huangshan factory we saw, men began the process, giving the teas an initial fixing by pressing them gently with their palms over hot woks. Several well-calibrated machines then finished the job. A series of high partitions rocked the leaves back and forth like a baby in a cradle, to dry out the tea. This last agitator also gave the tea its characteristic slight curve, while preserving the down.

While not quite as famous as Lung Ching, Huangshan Mao Feng is one of China's most celebrated green teas. Commonly found in the better tea markets around China, Huangshan Mao Feng became a tribute tea during the Qing dynasty. It is such an ancient tea, it was no surprise to find that so many people in the area still know how to make the tea by hand. In a system unique to China, where notions of private property are less strongly held, tea farms and factories regularly allow employees to take small amounts of the harvest to make tea for themselves. While passing through the village, Marcus and I saw several people making tea in their houses; in the restaurant where we stopped for dinner, we found the cook in the kitchen making Huangshan Mao Feng by hand to sell for spending cash. Handmade Huangshan is so rare, it is now a popular gift among businessmen. The factory managers with us gladly bought a few ounces.

The cook let me try my hand at shaping the leaves, showing me how to move the tea against the metal to get the leaves in a straight line. It looked easy, but I made a hash of it; I couldn't give the leaves any shape at all. His work was sublime, creating far more beautiful, downy leaves than the factory produced. For a moment I entertained thoughts of sourcing handmade Huangshan Mao Feng. I asked him how much he could make an hour. Once upon a time, tea factories employed hundreds of men shaping tea over woks just like this. Today, handmade Huangshan is a luxury few can afford. He explained that six hours of work would yield half a kilo of finished tea. I buy roughly thirty kilos of Huangshan a year. He would need two months to make that much, but the harvest itself lasts only ten days. When I brewed his tea, I was relieved to discover that its refinements did not merit its price. The equipment tea makers have designed to replace human hands approximates his work closely enough.

TAIPING HOUKUI
Taiping Best Monkey Tea

BREWING TEMPERATURE	175°F.
BREWING TIME	2–3 minutes.
DRY LEAVES	Taiping HouKui's thin, stiff, and fragile leaves are remarkably long—2 to 3 inches. Their incredibly bright shades of green—from iridescent chartreuse to dark emerald—are offset by little bits of dark white from the tips and sometimes a red lining. The leaves are imprinted with a fine cross-hatching pattern.
LIQUOR	Pale light green.
AROMAS	The honey and sweet floral notes of violets, with a vegetal undertone of wet hay and steamed green beans.
BODY	Medium.
FLAVORS	Not as sweet as the aroma—mellower and more rounded. Not quite as floral or light a finish as Pan Long; the tea has more vegetal notes of green beans or very fresh lima beans, and some "heat" flavors of toasted pecans.

Fitting Taiping HouKui's long, slender leaves into a brewing vessel feels like sliding spaghetti into a pot. Shaped like no other tea, the leaves yield a brew characteristic of the middle range of Chinese greens—slightly evocative of steamed cabbage, but with a sweet finish like spring honey. Taiping HouKui comes out of Anhui province, one of the few teas in this book from China's interior. The best comes from the town of Taiping, set on the steep banks of the river that flows from Taiping Lake, in the shadow of the Yellow Mountains, where Huangshan Mao Feng comes from.

This special tea is made from its own cultivar, bred for long leaves. The leafsets are plucked as late as possible, usually in late April, to give the leaves plenty of time to grow. After a quick fixing to retain the bright green color, the leaves are layered between yards of canvas, then weighted to compress the tea and flatten it into thin ribbons. In the process, the leaves pick up the imprint of the fabric. If you look carefully, you will see elegant small hatch marks on the leaves.

DRAGON PEARL JASMINE

BREWING TEMPERATURE	180°F.
BREWING TIME	3 minutes.
DRY LEAVES	Enchanting rolled pearls, marbled with strains of sage green and pearl white.
LIQUOR	Pale green.
AROMAS	Intoxicating, intense jasmine aromas, backed by sweet honey notes.
BODY	Surprisingly filling.
FLAVORS	Like liquid jasmine flowers, though mellower than the sharp aromas, the tea presents a wonderful blend of sweet honey and fresh floral flavors.

Now that you are familiar with pure Chinese green teas, having tasted a spectrum of them, you can experience the effect a classic addition can have on the brew. Dragon Pearl Jasmine draws most of its flavors not from the tea, but from the jasmine blossoms that perfume it.

For centuries, the Chinese have scented teas with fruits and flowers like dried lychees, rose petals, and osmanthus blossoms (see "Osmanthus," page 88). Tea makers generally fold in the additives to burnish teas lacking charms of their own. Cheap jasmine teas of this sort are ubiquitous at American Chinese restaurants. Dragon Pearl Jasmine is no cheap tea, but a haute version much beloved, in which jasmine flowers subtly infuse a tippy green tea full of character—and plenty of prized tips, or buds.

This tea is made in northern Fujian province, outside of the industrial city of Fu'an. The tea is made from the *Da Bai* ("big white") cultivar, famous for its large buds (see "Yin Zhen," page 21). The tea is harvested in early spring, when its large white tips are flush with flavor compounds the plant has stored over the winter. The leaves are fixed green, then dried and stored until around June, when the fragrant tiny jasmine flowers bloom. The blossoms are so fragrant, gathering them is a job I would happily accept. As soon as they are harvested, the flowers are rushed to the factories in Fu'an.

What happens next depends upon the factory. I had the chance to visit one factory in Fu'an; though I had to leave before the tea had finished infusing, I loved watching the preparations. At many tea factories, men work the tea wearing T-shirts and flip-flops to stay cool in the heat of the woks and dryers. Here, about twenty women in neat uniforms sat at tables equipped with bright lights. The women took small handfuls of the dried tea, which had been humidified to make the leaves pliable. They rolled the bud sets of a few leaves and a tip between their palms to form neat little pearls. Then they spread out the pearled leaves on trays. The trays were slid onto racks, alternating with trays of fresh-picked jasmine blossoms. The racks were stored in a small enclosed space for several days, with fresh flowers brought in every day, until the pearls were suffused with jasmine flavor. The tea would not be ready until several weeks after my departure, but I looked forward to receiving samples of the pearls when I purchased the tea later that spring.

Dragon Pearl Jasmine has recently become a very popular tea, and so it should be, as it represents the finest in Chinese handmade tea traditions. The tea is beautiful just to look at, with its small, dark green balls accented by light gray strands. The pearls contain a delicious floral aroma and sublime sweet flavor that cannot be compared with the artificial flavor of most jasmine teas. Just as vanilla extract cannot compare with the depth and butteriness of a real vanilla bean, man-made jasmine lacks the full spectrum of delicious floral notes that real jasmine blossoms provide.

GUNPOWDER

BREWING TEMPERATURE	175°F.
BREWING TIME	3–4 minutes.
DRY LEAVES	Dark green and tightly rolled, like something that might be shot out of a musket; the smaller and more tightly rolled, the better.
LIQUOR	Varies from a bright yellow to light brown to a green; the greener the liquor, the rounder and less acrid the flavors.
AROMAS	A definite aroma of burnt wood, even ash; definitely charred, though lacking the piney smokiness of Lapsang Souchong.
BODY	Medium.
FLAVORS	The charred, barely vegetal flavor of heavily grilled leeks.

When I tell tea brokers in China that I sell Gunpowder in the United States, they usually laugh; they assume this charred green tea makes its way only to North Africa and the Middle East. For centuries, Gunpowder has served as the base for Arabian mint tea, sweetened with plenty of sugar. Its strong, charred flavors taste wonderful with mint, but the tea is also delicious on its own.

Gunpowder is the only tea in this chapter that is not a Qing Ming, or spring, tea; since it gets all its flavors from its processing methods, the tea does not require leaves with much inherent strength. It is made from tougher and less tender later-season leaves, foliage that has grown almost twice as long as the leaves plucked earlier in the spring. The leaves are fixed and then fired for an extended period in a hot oven until they become shiny and slightly burnt. The oven is designed like a Laundromat dryer, tumbling the leaves over and over in a hot metal cylinder.

Gunpowder is produced almost entirely for export. For many years one of the only green teas available in the United States, it has been produced for more than two hundred years near coastal trading ports like Ningbo and in its ancestral home of Zhejiang province. The tea most likely gets its name from the shape of its leaves, so tightly rolled that they resemble the pellets soldiers once used as musket shot. (To those who have never seen a musket, the shiny gray green pellets also look like dried peas.) With its balled form and heavy firing, Gunpowder is among the most stable teas for transport, ideal for export in the age before vacuum packaging and airplanes. Unlike delicate, lightly fired Qing Ming teas, which lose their flavors quickly if not sealed, this tea arrived in good condition even after a year's sailboat journey from China to Great Britain. If the tea held any defects, its intensely smoky aromas usually covered them up.

Today, the tea is made in most provinces of China. Indeed, after the Qing Ming harvest, many tea farmers turn the rest of the year's new leaves into Gunpowder. As a result, there are many styles and many quality levels. The worst Gunpowder is bright yellow and acrid with smoky flavors; the best has charred but assuredly green, vegetal flavors.

JAPANESE GREEN TEAS

ith their vivid dark leaves and intensely green liquors, Japanese green teas have the heft of a thick vegetable broth and the deep, vegetal flavors of steamed spinach, sautéed green bell peppers, and sometimes nori seaweed. Before World War II brought an end to the trade, Japanese green teas made up an incredible 40 percent of all the tea imported by the United States. That trade has never resumed; today the Japanese drink almost all the teas made in Japan. It's a shame so little makes it off the islands, because these teas are delicious.

These teas are wonderful palate builders if only because the differences among them can be so subtle. They require a taster's full attention. In every way Chinese green teas vary, Japanese green teas can be remarkably alike. Indeed, the very phrase

Japanese green teas is redundant, because green is the only color of tea found in Japan.

Whereas China's tea industry has experienced perennial innovation and upheaval, tea makers in the small nation of Japan have adhered to the same production methods for almost the last two hundred years—in the case of Matcha tea, for the last five hundred. Some tea companies around the Japanese city of Uji have been producing tea since the 1600s. That kind of continuity doesn't exist in China or anywhere else in the world.

If anything has changed since tea first arrived from China in the ninth century, it is that the teas have become more uniform. While today the Chinese make tea from at least six hundred cultivars, the Japanese concentrate on just one. The *yabukita* clone was introduced in 1954 and now grows in over 90 percent of Japan's tea farms. The varietal produces a greater concentration of certain compounds called "amino acids" that give Japanese teas much of their characteristic brothiness, or *umami*.

While the Chinese draw on an arsenal of methods to fix their teas—woks, wood fires, charcoal, hot air, steam, or some combination, each creating distinct flavors—the Japanese use only hot water. Chinese tea makers manipulate their leaves to form every shape from snail shells to plum blossoms, and invent new forms all the time. Those Japanese tea makers who don't follow the thousand-year tradition of milling their leaves into Matcha powder follow the more recent Sencha leaf-rolling method—invented in 1740.

Tea first arrived in Japan from China in the 800s but did not take hold until the 1100s, when monks brought tea from the Jin Shan area in China to Japan's imperial capital of Kyoto. The tea was powdered following a Chinese fashion of the time. This precursor to modern-day Matcha powder was quickly adopted as a ceremonial beverage by both Japanese monasteries and the imperial court in Kyoto. The rest of society adopted a crude pan-roasted tea they called Bancha (unrelated to the modern tea drink of the same name). What we now know as the Japanese

JAPAN

Japan Boundary
River/Lake
Mountain Range

National Capital
City or Town

© 2008 Meighan Cavanaugh

Sea of Japan

Japan

Pacific Ocean

KYOTO
UJI
TOKYO
KAKEGAWA

KAGOSHIMA

N

tea ceremony was codified by the mid-sixteenth century, an hours-long production involving the careful preparation of Matcha tea. By the mid-seventeenth century, however, with the restrictions on Matcha lifted, a sort of middle class had emerged that was interested in a quicker, more everyday brew. Soen Nagatani, one of the tea manufacturers at Uji at that time, invented a technique of loose green tea production called the Sencha rolling method. This new system produced a brothy, mellow tea, one that quickly became the everyday tea of choice.

The Sencha rolling method is now practiced throughout Japan. After a brief steaming, the damp leaves are scattered on a bamboo surface to begin to dry out and cool off. The cooling leaves are then rolled with increasing amounts of pressure, breaking them up into more slender spears. These leaf fragments are by turns straightened and dried out in several stages. As with harvesting, almost all this rolling is now done by machine; it is still possible to find hand-rolled tea, but it is rare and expensive.

After rolling and drying, the teas are fired in a hot oven. This firing releases a number of roasted aroma compounds that give the teas a slightly sweet edge. The sweetness is extremely faint compared with the honeyed quality of many Chinese green teas. Japanese green teas have something of a caramelized, meaty bite behind their vegetal flavors, tasting a little bit like the crisp skin off of a roasted chicken. The best teas plucked in the spring have the most compounds and therefore the strongest roasted flavors.

Uji is Japan's oldest tea-growing region, having supplied tea since the 1100s to Japan's imperial capital of Kyoto and to the area's magnificent Buddhist monasteries. Uji still creates all of Japan's finest teas. Now that it is the suburb of an affluent city, its few remaining tea farms are endangered by sprawl; many farmers have sold their gardens to restaurant franchises and shopping malls. But in the eighteenth and nineteenth centuries, Uji tea farmers created not only the Sencha rolling method, but also the two principal sources of variation in Japanese teas: Sencha sun-grown teas and Gyokuro shade-grown teas.

Who came up with the idea of growing tea in the shade is lost to time, but we do know that shade builds up the levels of both chlorophyll and amino acids in the leaves, while lowering the polyphenols, giving the teas a darker, more vivid emerald hue and a smoother, more mellow and less astringent flavor than teas grown entirely in the sun. The leaves were once covered over with straw, and now are covered with black plastic, for anywhere from a few days to a few weeks before harvest. Gyokuro, Tencha, and Matcha are also shade-grown and often have a quality known to the Japanese as *umami,* for their mouth-filling richness.

With slightly lower levels of amino acids and chlorophyll and higher levels of certain polyphenols, sun-grown teas are lighter in color, more vegetal, and a little more astringent. There are two varieties of sun-grown teas: Sencha and Bancha. Growing on the same bush, Sencha—which means simply "New Tea"—consists of the smaller, tenderer leaves that emerge first; Bancha is made from the larger, older leaves that follow after the Sencha leaves have been plucked. There are several harvests of each: After the First Sencha and the First Bancha, the shorn, stunted tea plants regrow, creating a fresh crop of small leaves for a Second Sencha, followed by another round of larger leaves for a Second Bancha, and so forth. Three Sencha harvests per year is considered ideal to allow for the healthiest, most robust First Sencha the following year.

Japan's First Senchas, just like China's Qing Ming teas and India's First Flush Darjeelings, are particularly exquisite because they contain the best of the compounds the plant has stored over the winter. The First Sencha harvest can last over a week or two. Extending the theory that earlier is better, Ichiban Senchas are particularly prized, as they are made from the very first leaves plucked during the first day or two of the First Sencha harvest.

Senchas have become so popular in Japan that the tea is now produced on a mass scale, often in lesser quality. Since World War II, a "deep steaming" method called *fukamushi* has been invented that breaks up the leaves into even finer filaments. These particles give the tea a stronger, less nuanced flavor and allow it to be brewed more quickly for people on the go. Of even greater concern, the demand for Sencha has begun to outpace supply, so much so that the Japanese have begun importing Japanese-style Senchas grown in China and passing them off as Japanese. Largely because of a lack of experience as well as inferior soil, these Chinese Senchas are usually dramatically inferior: grassy, yellow, and often harshly astringent. Generic Sencha teas sometimes contain some Chinese Sencha and are almost always made of a blend of the entire year's harvests, not just the best from the spring. High-end Senchas like the three in this book are 100 percent Japanese and contain only the first spring leaves.

For the purposes of your palate, I recommend tasting the teas in this chapter in one of two ways: all at once, if possible, or in three groups of three. The first three are Senchas. The next three are Banchas. The final three are all grown in the shade. Because all nine are made up of much finer leaf particles relative to the more whole-leaf Chinese green teas, they can be brewed for as little as one minute, at between 160 and 175 degrees Fahrenheit.

MATSUDA'S SENCHA

BREWING TEMPERATURE	175°F.
BREWING TIME	1–2 minutes.
DRY LEAVES	Vivid, forest green, fine, slender spears about 1 inch long, shiny and silken.
LIQUOR	Intense yellow green.
AROMAS	Vibrant, with fresh lemon notes backed by a nice spinachy aroma and the roasted hints of nori seaweed.
BODY	Medium light; mouth-fillingly brothy.
FLAVORS	Vegetal, opening with sautéed chard and resolving to roasted nori seaweed. The sweetest of the three Senchas, the tea's pale sweet sheen is balanced by a slight bitterness on the back of the tongue. The sweetness endures and evolves long after you've sipped the tea.

Sencha is the finest expression of green tea, and Matsuda's intensely brothy, vibrant brew is among the finest expressions of Sencha. Yoshihiro Matsuda lives in Japan's great Uji tea region. His farm has been in his family for many generations, a small plot set halfway up a sloping hillside. It is unusual to find a farmer who makes the tea from start to finish; most growers in Japan—as in the rest of the world—take the tea only to a certain point, then sell it to processors to finish it. Matsuda, his wife, and his mother make and finish their exquisite green tea from beginning to end.

As a tea importer, I visit a lot of farms. Although they are fun to see, they usually don't tell me much about the quality of the tea, as too much happens between the plant and the tin. Matsuda tends his fields with such care, his tea leaves are noticeably bigger, juicier, greener, and sweeter than those grown by his neighbors on the same hillside. While his neighbors use shading to make Kabuse Sencha, an innovation increasingly popular in the Uji region, Matsuda never covers his plants; he considers shading a shortcut, an unnatural flavor enhancer that boosts the amino acid content of the leaves by hiding the sun. He prefers to boost the nutrient content of his leaves by nourishing them with healthy soil and plenty of sun.

As Matsuda's tea leaves have more amino acids and sugars than most, his tea's aromas and flavors are also more luscious, intense, rounded, and sweet. He enhances those qualities at each step in the tea making. After carefully plucking his leaves with small, handheld hedge trimmers, Matsuda lets them wither for a very short period on a tarp, where they acquire the lemony, vegetal aromatic compounds called "linalools" and "hexanols." Then he fixes his teas for the traditional time of thirty seconds, keeping his leaves more whole. (Deep-steamed, or *fukamushi*, Senchas get sixty to ninety seconds and fall apart into smaller filaments, creating a more assertive but less nuanced tea.) To further preserve the teas' aromas, Matsuda rolls the leaves firmly but not excessively, giving them a duller finish than most Japanese Senchas, which are ordinarily shiny and polished from heavier rolling. Finally, Matsuda fires the tea lightly in an oven, creating a slight roasted or toasty aroma layered over the lemony, lush flavors of the leaves. The result is an exquisite, almost pastoral Sencha. Like a classic Barolo, Matsuda's Sencha is structured and refined, its vegetal base notes reined in by high fresh lemon and roasted flavors.

KAKEGAWA ICHIBAN SENCHA

BREWING TEMPERATURE	175°F.
BREWING TIME	1–3 minutes.
DRY LEAVES	A fine mix of leaf filaments; lighter and more powdery than the forest green needles of Matsuda's Sencha, Kakegawa's finer particles are a matte sage green.
LIQUOR	Intense, almost neon green; a little clouded from the fine leaf particles.
AROMAS	The dark vegetal aromas of cooked spinach and nori seaweed and the fainter citrusy top note of lemon juice.
BODY	Medium; somewhat sharp and astringent.
FLAVORS	Bracing: lemony at the start, with the bite of cooked spinach in the finish. Among the most assertive Senchas here, with the intensity and astringency (almost guttiness) of its deep-steamed flavor.

This bracing, lemony tea is an assertive example of a popular modern style of Japanese green tea, *fukamushi* Ichiban Sencha. Unlike the previous Sencha made exclusively by Yoshihiro Matsuda, Kakegawa Ichiban Sencha is actually a blend of teas grown from the same area, Shizuoka, located a few hours east of Uji. Ichiban means "the first," indicating the tea was produced from the first, most tender leaves harvested at the beginning of May.

Uji produces Japan's very finest teas but accounts for only 3 percent of the country's total production. Today, close to 50 percent of Japan's teas come from a fertile wedge on the coastal hills south of the city of Shizuoka, in the shadows of Mount Fuji, about an hour south of Tokyo.

The hills surrounding Kakegawa are covered with tea plants, perfectly manicured rows of green. The area is so dominated by tea production that one hill has a tea bush topiary trimmed in the shape of the Japanese character for tea. The tea operations here are among the most sophisticated in the world. The hills are outfitted with a network of huge metal fans that protect the tea from frost (the fans keep the cold air from settling low near the leaves, where they could kill the young tender shoots). The tea factories are spread out every couple of miles throughout the region, all ready to process the harvest quickly.

Kakegawan tea makers first developed the *fukamushi* style of Sencha that I described in the introduction to this chapter. The *fukamushi* method of deep steaming was invented after World War II to improve the quality of tea massproduced from larger, poorer leaves. While lasting only thirty seconds longer than traditional steaming, deep steaming breaks up the leaves into much smaller filaments, allowing for a stronger and quicker brew. Compared with the refined, polished, almost pastoral quality of Matsuda's Sencha, Kakegawa Ichiban Sencha has all the punch and intensity of Tokyo at rush hour. The Japanese have so come to enjoy the flavors of *fukamushi* Sencha that almost all Sencha in Japan today is deep-steamed.

KAGOSHIMA SENCHA

BREWING TEMPERATURE	175°F.
BREWING TIME	1–2 minutes.
DRY LEAVES	Silky, semiglossy mix of *fukamushi* filaments and Sencha-rolled stiff, forest green needles.
LIQUOR	Pale light green.
AROMAS	Higher-pitched than the previous two Senchas, with a fresh lemony note above a base vegetal mixture of cooked spinach and bell peppers.
BODY	Medium; somewhat astringent.
FLAVORS	More vegetal than the aroma, with the angular, assertive flavor of green bell peppers and the rounded, roasted flavor of toasted walnuts.

This lively, vegetal, but high-pitched tea is a vivid illustration of a good-quality blended Sencha. Kagoshima is a port city on the southern tip on Japan's Kyushu island, the second largest tea-producing area in Japan after Shizuoka. Kyushu is also the southernmost tea-producing area in Japan. Spring comes earlier here than to the rest of Japan's tea regions, so Kyushu brings Japan its first spring teas.

The island's large, flat plateau allows for Japan's biggest tea farms. The farms are vast and flat enough to accommodate an unusual harvesting system: Giant tractors ride up and down the rows, trimming the newest leaves like outsize lawn mowers and blowing cuttings into large bags behind them.

This mechanical harvest allows for such economies of scale that Kagoshima produces the cheapest teas in all of Japan. But the scope of these operations also prevents the gardens from making great pure Senchas. Instead of nurturing exquisite Senchas from just one field or cultivar, as Yoshihiro Matsuda can do in Uji with his premium Matsuda's Sencha, Kagoshima tea makers blend one great Sencha from several varieties of individually inferior plants. One is what's called a "natural Gyokuro" Sencha. Its leaves flourish entirely in the sun but still produce the extra amino acids of a shade-grown tea. The result of this blending is a lemony Sencha with some of the rich, vegetal brothiness of a Gyokuro.

BANCHA

BREWING TEMPERATURE	175°F.
BREWING TIME	1–3 minutes.
DRY LEAVES	Unlike Senchas, with their slender emerald needles, Bancha consists of comparatively wide leaves mixed with stalks, ranging in color from sage green to khaki.
LIQUOR	Bright yellow.
AROMAS	A lively, grassier tea than Sencha, as though someone turned up the volume on Sencha's lemony notes, but with subtle green tea base notes of spinach and nori, along with faint hints of toasted walnuts.
BODY	Light.
FLAVORS	Lighter vegetal flavors of grass, celery, and wet wood.

It's amazing what a difference a few weeks makes. Bancha is made of the larger, tougher leaves that emerge just fifteen to twenty days after the younger Sencha shoots have been harvested. As the season wears on, the chemical composition of the leaves also changes. By the time the Bancha harvest begins, the better, smoother-tasting polyphenols in the leaves have been replaced by poorer, harsher ones, and the leaves have lost a great deal of their amino acid content. Bancha therefore yields a higher-pitched, more lemony, lighter-bodied tea.

Bancha grows everywhere Sencha does, in Uji, Shizuoka, and Kyushu. But lacking Sencha's premium qualities, Bancha is not distinguished by grower or region but is blended together under the generic term. The leaves are processed the way Senchas are—steam-fixed, rolled in several stages, and then dried in an oven. Yet the result has a completely different character; Bancha is something of a brassy adolescent next to the mature, restrained Sencha. On a superficial level, tougher Bancha leaves remain whole even if deep-steamed, unlike Sencha leaves, which fall apart into small filaments if steamed for more than half a minute. While still a lovely everyday tea, and a wonderful base for iced teas, Bancha also helps elucidate the comparative finesse and brothy mouth-filling pleasures of Sencha.

GENMAICHA

BREWING TEMPERATURE	190°F.
BREWING TIME	1–3 minutes.
DRY LEAVES	Broad, yellowish Bancha tea leaves mixed with toasted brown rice, some crunchy whole kernels and some popped like baby popcorn. There are many styles of GenMaiCha, so the size of the tea leaf and the percentage of open rice kernels vary widely.
LIQUOR	Vibrant light green.
AROMAS	Pleasant, rounded smell of roasted rice.
BODY	Light.
FLAVORS	Above a baseline vegetal flavor of spring grass, the strong roasted flavor of toasted rice, somewhat evocative of popcorn but without the corn sweetness.

GenMaiCha is a creative use of Bancha tea and an eloquent unification of the two crops central to Japanese culture: tea and rice. The light-bodied roasted tea is a blend of *genmai*, or unpolished brown rice, and *cha*, or Bancha tea. For centuries, the two commodities have been staples of the Japanese diet. In the 1920s, a clever Kyoto tea merchant combined the two to make this blend.

Once considered a cheap peasant beverage, GenMaiCha has recently come into vogue among Japanese urban elite and in the United States as a health drink.

The tea comes in many grades and styles but always consists of Bancha and roasted rice. The roasted flavors of the two components complement each other: The lemony Bancha helps sweeten the rice, and the nutty rice helps mellow out the often grassy tea.

HOJICHA

BREWING TEMPERATURE	190°F.
BREWING TIME	1–3 minutes.
DRY LEAVES	No leaves at all; just small, light brown wooden stalks resembling chopped-up toothpicks.
LIQUOR	Caramel brown.
AROMAS	Gently reminiscent of roasted coffee, with sweet caramel notes.
BODY	Medium strong.
FLAVORS	Notes of wood and toasted nuts; while not sweet in the beginning, it yields to a nice caramel finish, evocative of molasses and burnt marshmallows.

Another creative use of tea by-products, Hojicha is made almost entirely of the leafless stalks that come off with the leaves when tea plants are harvested mechanically. Hojicha did not exist before mechanical harvesters were invented; hand harvesters simply left the stalks on the plants, taking only the leaves. Today, Bancha has to be mechanically harvested three times a year to ensure the best quality of the prime spring Sencha crop the following year. That means a lot of twigs. The twigs can be drunk green or roasted, but I prefer the roasted style.

As with Sencha and Gyokuro teas, the tea-growing region of Uji was the source of this innovation. In the 1920s, an entrepreneurial merchant started roasting twigs and selling them in Kyoto, making a profit from something tea makers had until then considered waste.

Like fresh-roasted coffee in specialty food stores, Hojicha is often set out in many Japanese food stores to lure in shoppers with its delicious roasted aromas. In fact, Hojicha tastes so much like coffee, it might be the ideal cup to wean a coffee lover off that cruder rival brew.

GYOKURO

BREWING TEMPERATURE	160°F.
BREWING TIME	1–3 minutes.
DRY LEAVES	Shiny, emerald green spindles.
LIQUOR	Pale green.
AROMAS	Very spinachy and seaweedy, dark and decidedly vegetal, with none of the lemon sheen of Sencha. Lovely and soothing, like a hearty spinach soup simmering on the kitchen stove.
BODY	Medium; fuller-bodied for a green tea, with a mild astringent bite.
FLAVORS	The lush green flavor of the freshest steamed spinach, the cooked flavor of toasted walnuts, and a very slight note of sulfur. Filling and sustaining. Praised for its consistency; unlike in most other good-quality teas, the flavor does not evolve much but holds steady as you swirl it in your mouth.

Like most great things Japanese, Gyokuro is a study in subtlety. A type of tea as well as an adjective, it has come to describe teas with *umami,* or mouth-coating sensation, as that caused by this lovely shade-grown tea. Judging the gentle differences that shade growing makes requires careful attention. Though Gyokuro tea grows partially in the shade, and Sencha teas grow in the sun, both are processed the same way. The leaves therefore resemble each other closely, both in appearance and in taste. Yet the shade covering of Gyokuro accounts for a subtly lusher, darker, more mouth-coating tea.

Most Gyokuro is grown around Uji, half an hour south of the former capital of Kyoto. The shade-growing method was developed at the end of the Edo era, in the 1860s. Once a rural suburb of Kyoto, Uji has now become quite busy. Apartment houses and office buildings have replaced many Gyokuro tea fields. The remaining fields that make Gyokuro are wedged in between the buildings and on the hills that surround the city. About three weeks before the May harvest, the gardens are shaded over. They were once covered in rice straw; today growers use black plastic mesh.

Since the gardens are so small, crops are usually plucked by hand. Then the leaves are promptly steam-fixed to preserve the lovely dark green color of the leaves. Following the Sencha rolling method, the leaves pass through a series of machines that shape and dry the leaves in stages, approximating the steps skilled handlers once followed to make hand-rolled Gyokuro. (Since it takes about four hours to make a kilo of hand-rolled Gyokuro, it is rare to find hand-rolled tea, but the very long and slender leaves make a light, elegant brew.) After the rolling, the tea is dried in an oven. The result is a special tea the Japanese particularly prize for its constant, vegetal flavor with gentle, soothing roasted notes.

TENCHA

BREWING TEMPERATURE	150°F.
BREWING TIME	1–3 minutes.
DRY LEAVES	A mix of green and yellow, round, ragged leaf particles.
LIQUOR	Light yellow green.
AROMAS	A light vegetal aroma of steamed spinach and steamed artichoke hearts, with the slight sweetness of steamed white rice.
BODY	Medium; fuller for a green tea, with a mild astringent bite.
FLAVORS	A soft, spinachy flavor with the rounded sweetness of steamed white rice and none of the roasted flavors of nuts or nori seaweed.

With its clean vegetal flavors of steamed spinach and artichoke hearts and a pleasant medium body, Tencha makes for a wonderful tutor. Unlike every other tea we've tasted so far in this chapter, it is not rolled and dried according to the Sencha rolling method, nor is it fired in a hot oven. Merely chopped up and air-dried, Tencha offers one of the purest expressions of mature tea leaves. Tencha has no roasted flavors, only pure vegetal notes of steamed artichokes cooked in lemon water. It makes for a wonderful comparison with the roasted flavors of the other great green teas, Japanese and Chinese alike.

Tencha is a shade-grown tea like Gyokuro, covered over during the last three weeks before the early May harvest. The best Tencha comes from the Uji tea fields in Kyoto prefecture, where it originated, as well as from Mie prefecture to the southeast. Immediately after harvesting, the teas are steam-fixed to preserve their brilliant green color. Unlike Gyokuro or Sencha, Tencha leaves are not rolled; they are merely chopped up and then placed in a cylinder, where they are blown with warm air. Tencha is hardly ever drunk in Japan; the leaves are usually ground into Matcha powder. Though rare, Tencha makes for a delightfully light, refreshing cup of tea.

MATCHA

BREWING TEMPERATURE	175°F.
BREWING TIME	30 seconds of fast whisking.
DRY LEAVES	A fine powder, almost neon green.
LIQUOR	Thick, frothy, opaque, and bright green.
AROMAS	The aromas are faint, discernible only from the broth: They offer a hint of honeydew melon sweetness over a base note of cooked spinach.
BODY	Thick, bracing, drying the mouth.
FLAVORS	A mouth-filling, even head-filling, broth. The flavors of Tencha amplified exponentially, Matcha tastes intensely of spinach and artichokes, followed by a bracing caffeine bite.

Heady and intense, Matcha offers a tea experience like no other. The only tea in this book made from powdered leaves, dissolved Matcha yields smooth vegetal flavors with a surprisingly bitter but satisfying kick. The better Matchas balance the bitterness with sweet notes—especially in the aftertaste, which should linger long in the back of the mouth.

Matcha is made from Tencha (see page 70). The leaves are shaded over a few weeks before harvest to boost their chlorophyll, amino acids, and other flavor compounds. Then the leaves are steam-fixed, cut, and air-dried rather than rolled and fired. This gives them a lovely, clean vegetal flavor unvarnished with any roasted sweetness.

Unlike Tencha, which is left whole, Matcha is then milled into a fine powder. Today, traditional stone mills have given way to impressive high-tech operations. I had the chance to visit one factory and had to don protective clothing as if heading into surgery. I even had to pause in an airlock where machines blew off from the protective clothing any particulate matter that might contaminate the powder. In the production room, everything was covered with bright green dust, especially the rows upon rows of millstones whirring away. The millstones have their work cut out for them: After a full hour of grinding, they produce only two ounces of the powdered tea.

There are several levels of Matcha. The best is called *koicha,* or "thick tea." Made from the best spring leaves harvested in Uji, *koicha* is ordinarily reserved for tea ceremonies. The next level down is called *usucha,* or "thin tea." *Usucha* is less expensive, making it more suitable for everyday use. A third commercial grade is used for ice cream, lattes, and other green tea flavorings. As with Sencha, the demand for Matcha is now great enough that some is made in China, a curious reversal of history given that powdered tea had not been made in China since the Ming dynasty, which ended in 1644.

The oldest type of tea found in Japan, Matcha is what Buddhist monks brought back with them to Kyoto after visiting the Jin Shan monastery in the ninth century (see "Jin Shan," page 35). After monks began cultivating tea in Japan, the Matcha they made was consumed mostly by monks and royalty, then trickled down only as far as the noble warrior class, the samurai. The preparation of powdered Matcha became ritualized in the 1550s by a Japanese tea master named Sen Rikyu, who codified the practice of Chado. Literally translated as "the Way of Tea," Chado is a form of religious observance as well as a tea ceremony. Influenced by Taoism as well as Zen Buddhism, Rikyu ritualized the tea service as a means of drawing attention to the beauty and purity of everyday objects. By indicating the proper tools and gestures to use while brewing and serving the tea, as well as the arrangement and architecture of the teahouse, Rikyu encouraged practitioners to focus on the elements involved in tea: water, fire, and the green tea itself. After his death, his three grandsons developed their own schools: Omotesenke, Urasenke, and Mushanokojisenke. Each of these schools still exists in Japan sixteen generations later.

There are many books on Chado; for our purposes, you do not need to perform a tea ceremony to cultivate a palate for Matcha. All you need to brew it is a deep-sided bowl and a fine whisk. The Japanese traditionally use a bamboo whisk called a "*chasen*," but a small metal whisk will do in a pinch. Warm the bowl with hot water, then carefully dry the bowl out to prevent the Matcha powder from clumping. Place 1 level teaspoon of Matcha powder in the bowl. Pour over 1 cup of water heated to 175 degrees Fahrenheit. Whisk the tea in brisk angular motions for 30 seconds, repeatedly tracing out an *M* in the cup to form a thick, foamy broth. Take a sip; the broth will fill your mouth with sensation. As the initial impact begins to fade, you should be able to detect vegetal flavors of spinach along with the gently bitter bite of the caffeine.

OOLONGS

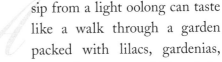

A sip from a light oolong can taste like a walk through a garden packed with lilacs, gardenias, and jasmine. A darker oolong can smell like a bakery right after it's finished a round of peach pies. Oolongs are some of my favorite teas. From their own cultivar of *Camellia sinensis* and their singular methods of production, oolongs take on an astonishing array of flavors and aromas. Many oolongs are creamy, their liquor literally coating your mouth like fresh cream. Others are almost effervescent, practically fizzing like Champagne. Their variety of colors is lovely to behold, from the pale greenish yellow liquor of Ti Guan Yin to the dark orange brew of Fenghuang ShuiXian.

Oolongs bridge the divide between green and black teas. The process that turns teas black is

TEA	OXIDATION LEVEL*
Wenshan BaoZhong	
Ali Shan	25%
Dong Ding	
Ti Guan Yin	
Osmanthus	
Fenghuang ShuiXian	40%
Bai Hao (Fanciest Formosa Oolong)	75%
Da Hong Pao	
Formosa Oolong	

These are my estimations from my own experience.

called "oxidation"; I've explained its particulars in an appendix on the manufacture of tea entitled "From Tree to Tea" (page 193). Suffice to say, if green teas are not oxidized at all, and black teas are 100 percent oxidized, oolongs range from 10 to 75 percent.

To carry you from the green teas of the previous chapter to the Chinese black teas to come, I have arranged these oolongs according to their oxidation levels.

We'll start with Wenshan BaoZhong, the lightest oolong, closest to a green tea. We'll end with Formosa Oolong, the darkest and nearest to black tea. Of the nine teas in this chapter, the first four teas, with their lighter levels of oxidation, have primarily citrus and floral flavors like lemon and gardenia. The last and darker five taste of stone fruits such as apricot and peach.

Oolongs likely first appeared within the last three to four hundred years in China's Fujian province, in the Wuyi Mountains. Presumably frustrated with the quality of their green teas, tea makers there found something to catch the attention of the emperor's tribute board when they decided not to fix their green teas but to let them wither and darken to black tea. Later, they figured out how to halt the oxidation by degrees, making the teas ever lighter in color. As you will taste, the results were magical. As this new tea's reputation spread, so too did its growing techniques. Oolong making spread south to the mountains in Guangdong province. Oolong makers from Fujian also began immigrating to Taiwan. (Taiwan lies directly across the Taiwan Strait from Fujian, and most of its residents speak the same Fujian dialect of Chinese.) Today, the best oolongs still come from China and Taiwan.

Oolongs have become truly exquisite in just the last twenty years. The same factors that have upturned the rest of the tea world have transformed these teas: vacuum packaging, air transport, and the reopening of the People's Republic of China to international trade in the 1970s. When the Communist country was under embargo in the 1950s and 1960s, Taiwanese tea makers made their fortunes producing ersatz versions of Lung Ching, Gunpowder, Ti Guan Yin, and other Mainland Chinese tea classics. When the embargo was lifted, cheaper and better versions suddenly became available from China itself. The Taiwanese were forced to grow something else. Luckily for us, they chose to grow oolongs. Capitalizing on the benefits of vacuum packaging and air shipping, they did away with the heavy firings once required to preserve and transport teas, creating oolongs of terrific lightness and nuance. They achieved such success that in just the last several years, a growing number of private Mainland Chinese tea makers have copied them, lightening and improving their oolongs in turn. As a result, today we have some of the freshest, most remarkable oolongs ever available. Five of the oolongs in this chapter come from Taiwan, and four come from China.

Since their flavors can be so complex, I suggest you drink oolongs later in the day, when you are awake enough to observe them. Then keep drinking them: Unlike most teas, oolongs can actually improve with multiple brewings. Both the Chinese and the Taiwanese like to drink oolongs *gong fu* style, brewing the tea in several rounds, using a small clay pot, then pouring the tea out into tiny ceramic cups and sipping it with six or seven friends.

To brew an oolong *gong fu* style, fill a small teapot with about 1½ to 2 tablespoons of tea. Rinse the leaves with lukewarm water, then brew them for 1 minute. Pour out the tea into small cups, then start a fresh pot with the same leaves while you drink the first round. Brew each subsequent pot for an additional 30 seconds. The flavors and aromas will continue to evolve through five to seven rounds before fading. If you do not have a group of friends available, all of these oolongs still taste marvelous brewed even just once.

WENSHAN BAOZHONG
Paper-Wrapped Oolong

BREWING TEMPERATURE	205° to 212°F.
BREWING TIME	2–4 minutes.
DRY LEAVES	Considering the light color of the liquor, the leaves are surprisingly dark: army green to black leaves, coiled tightly like thick segments of rope.
LIQUOR	Light gold.
AROMAS	The Taiwanese say BaoZhong is their most aromatic oolong. The tea is so fragrant, it is hard to stop smelling its blend of gardenia, jasmine, and butter aromas.
BODY	Medium, with some creaminess lightly coating the tongue.
FLAVORS	At its freshest, BaoZhong tastes of nothing but honeyed flowers. After a few brews, it loses some of that sheen and takes on a lovely seriousness. If the tea is more than a few months old, it begins to taste like a vegetal green tea.

As the "greenest" of the oolongs, Wenshan BaoZhong has a light green color and gentle floral flavors of gardenia and jasmine, making it an ideal oolong to start with after the green teas of the previous two chapters.

The way BaoZhong is made, every step results in a lighter, gentler, and greener oolong. First harvesters pluck tender leaves that are larger than most green teas but not as big or tough as most oolongs. Then the leaves are withered in the sun, but only briefly (fifteen to thirty minutes), where they wilt and begin to develop some of their aromas. After withering indoors for an additional half day, the leaves are placed in a heated tumbler resembling a clothes dryer. The hot air almost completely fixes the leaves, preserving their green color. The partially fixed leaves are then rolled. Since they are so tender, they cannot withstand the pressure needed to twist them into the more common oolong ball shape (see "Ali Shan," page 81). Instead, the leaves are rolled into tight coiled twists. The twisted leaves are left to oxidize, but only for a short time and only to 10 or 20 percent. Finally, the tea is fired only to stop the oxidation and to dry the tea for preservation, not to give it any smoky flavors.

One of the oldest Taiwanese oolongs, BaoZhong grows just outside bustling Taipei, the island's capital. The gardens lie to the south of the city, in a quiet mountainside spot where the air is clear of urban smog and mist almost always cloaks the gardens. For over 120 years, almost the length of Taiwanese tea history, the tiny town of PingLing has devoted itself to making BaoZhong for Chinese expatriates around the Pacific Rim. When the Japanese occupied Taiwan during World War II, they sent BaoZhong from Singapore to Saigon to Manila, often in beautiful paper wrappings decorated with lovely, intricate stamps.

PingLing is so tea centered, it boasts several tea factories, a tea museum, and even streetlights shaped like teapots. Restaurants here serve wonderful foods cooked in BaoZhong tea: pork belly braised in it, fresh trout poached in it, even tea puddings sweetened with BaoZhong and condensed milk. Before you cook with it, get to know its delicate floral flavors. They are some of the most refined in the world of oolongs.

ALI SHAN

Ali Mountain

BREWING TEMPERATURE	205° to 212°F.
BREWING TIME	3–4 minutes.
DRY LEAVES	A balled oolong, Ali Shan boasts leaves that are tight, shiny pellets of a surprisingly dark green-brown color, given the tea's light liquor.
LIQUOR	Light gold.
AROMAS	Potent gardenia and lilac aromas with top notes of crystallized sugar and fresh citrus, akin to key lime pie topped with meringue.
BODY	Medium light and creamy, filling the mouth.
FLAVORS	Among the creamiest of oolongs, Ali Shan gives a nice coating sensation and some butteriness along with lime citrus notes and a quiet, underlying vegetal flavor.

Creamy, citrusy, floral, and fragrant, Ali Shan is a prime example of what are called high-mountain oolongs from Taiwan.

High-mountain oolongs first emerged in the early 1980s, after the lifting of the embargo against world trade with Communist China. During the embargo, Taiwanese tea makers made a fine living selling ersatz versions of Chinese green teas to Chinese expatriates throughout South Asia. With the collapse of the market for their inferior versions of Chinese teas, in the early 1980s, a few intrepid tea makers from the nearby Dong Ding growing area experimented in the high mountains that form Taiwan's spine (see "Dong Ding," page 84). They found that the higher altitudes led to creamier and more floral teas.

Why the altitude does this is still up for debate. It seems likely the cooler temperatures and reduced sunshine in the misty mountains stunt the leaves' growth, concentrating their flavors. The cloud cover may also increase certain amino acids that give the tea its heavier, creamy body, a thickness in the mouth that evokes the coating feeling of heavy cream.

While Ali Shan now has competition from Li Shan, another high-altitude oolong grown on an even higher mountain a few hours away, Ali Shan was Taiwan's first high-altitude tea and remains among the finest. Named for the steep five-thousand-foot peak in southern Taiwan, the tea has a surprisingly delicate flavor given the hard work required for its production.

The tea bushes grow in rows on the steep sides of the mountain, terraced between lines of betel nut palms. Those tropical palms remind you how close you are to the equator, how far south you are from the more temperate tea-growing regions of China and Japan. The harvesters negotiate the inclines with their tea baskets, plucking the tea by hand, enduring intermittent blasts of rain and hot sun.

Weather permitting, the plucked tea is spread on a tarp in the sunshine, where the leaves develop their jasmine, rose, and geranium aromas. The tarp is periodically folded and unfolded to sift and slightly bruise the leaves, triggering oxidation. After about half an hour, the tea leaves are transferred to large bamboo trays to wither indoors for an additional eight hours. More and more Taiwanese oolong makers air-condition their withering rooms to help reduce the leaves' moisture content even further. The chilled air also improves the flavor by slowing down the oxidation.

Next the leaves are rolled and shaped into balls, a process far more arduous and time-consuming than the twisting of Wenshan BaoZhong (page 79) and other twisted oolongs. Makers of balled oolongs like Ali Shan drag out the rolling process over six to eight hours to deepen the floral aromas and flavors. They perform a dance perfected in China's Fujian province by makers of Ti Guan Yin (page 86). Strong men harness the withered leaves in large canvas bags. They use one machine alone just to cinch the bags tight until they look like giant spheres of cheesecloth-bound mozzarella. The workers then slip the bags between two spring-loaded rotating disks, whose turning action forces the leaves to ball up upon themselves. Once performed by human feet, the rolling also provokes oxidation by breaking down the leaves. To slow the oxidation, after only a few minutes, the men remove the bags from between the disks, untie them, and toss the leaves into a large rotating drum. The drum resembles a very long clothes dryer, but without the heat source; as it spins the leaves like so many tiny articles of clothing, it cools and dries them. To restart the oxidation, after a few minutes more, the men return the leaves from the dryer to the canvas bags. Then they cinch them again and slip them back inside the disks of the rolling machines.

Incredibly, they repeat this process up to thirty times over the space of six to eight hours. An exhausting dance, but well worth it: At the end of the day, the leaves look like tight balls the size of peas, fully dried and only 25 percent oxidized. The tea's extraordinary citrus scents and floral sweetness evoke fresh-bloomed gardenias and fresh-baked key lime pie.

DONG DING

Frozen Peak

BREWING TEMPERATURE	205° to 212°F.
BREWING TIME	3–4 minutes.
DRY LEAVES	Dark green leaves rolled into rough balls, most of them with a short piece of stem still attached.
LIQUOR	Light gold.
AROMAS	Sweet, with a mixture of gardenia and lemon taffy.
BODY	Medium body carrying no astringency.
FLAVORS	Creamy, like lemon taffy with the underlying vegetal characteristics of Chinese green teas.

Made almost like Ali Shan (page 81), Dong Ding is a lovely example of a creamy, lemony oolong, slightly darker than its high-mountain brethren and slightly more restrained. Along with Wenshan BaoZhong (page 79), Dong Ding is Taiwan's most famous and beloved oolong and most likely its first.

Tea makers have cultivated Dong Ding around the town of Luku in the foothills of Taiwan's famous Central Mountain Range since the mid-1800s. Whether Dong Ding came before Wenshan BaoZhong is a matter of some debate. Legend has it a tea maker from Fujian province in China made the short hop across the Taiwan Strait along with a dozen tea bushes, planting them at the base of Dong Ding Mountain. Tea makers quickly adopted the rolled-ball method used in Ti Guan Yin (page 81; for the rolled-ball method, see "Ali Shan," page 86).

While Dong Ding is grown within view of a snow-peaked mountain (hence its name), the tea is not considered a high-mountain oolong because of the mountain's lower elevation. Nonetheless, over the last twenty years, Dong Ding makers have begun imitating the high-altitude tea-making techniques, making their tea much lighter than they once did, oxidizing and firing the leaves for much shorter times. As a result, today's Dong Ding now resembles Ali Shan and Li Shan, but with a darker liquor and similar but more subdued floral and citrus flavors.

TI GUAN YIN
Iron Goddess of Mercy

BREWING TEMPERATURE	205° to 212°F.
BREWING TIME	3–4 minutes.
DRY LEAVES	Loosely balled leaves ranging from dark to bright green, with dabs of red along the leaves' edges and no stems.
LIQUOR	Golden yellow.
AROMAS	The scent of this tea reminds me of the fine Burgundian white wine Meursault; some also smell of lily of the valley and gardenias.
BODY	Medium.
FLAVORS	Floral gardenia notes, along with the fine, creamy sweetness of buttered white toast and a finish of cooked sugar like cotton candy.

With its spun-sugar finish and refined gardenia aromas, medium-bodied Ti Guan Yin is among the most heralded oolongs in the world, and rightfully so. Ti Guan Yin comes from the area in China's Fujian province where oolongs were first invented and may be the oldest known oolong as well as one of the very best. The best Ti Guan Yin I've ever bought comes from a small village about forty miles from the coast called XiPing (pronounced "Shee-Ping"). Tea gardens fill the steep hills rising from the river valley, along with elaborately ornamented houses with charming peaked roofs resembling the prows of old sailing ships. These wonderful houses are a testament to the prosperity Ti Guan Yin has given XiPing over the centuries.

Ti Guan Yin is one of the few teas said to be divinely inspired. Its creation myth holds that a farmer was renovating a temple to the Buddhist deity Guan Yin, a female bodhisattva of compassion, when her iron statue came to life. To thank him for cleaning her temple, she told him his fortune would be found in the fields right outside. There the farmer found a tea bush and named the tea he made with it after her.

Ti Guan Yin is typically harvested from middle to late May, when the leaves are more mature and fuller-sized than green tea leaves. After harvesting, the leaves are withered in the sun for thirty minutes, then gently agitated on a tarp in order to bruise them slightly. Then the tea is brought indoors to continue withering for an additional six hours. While originally a twisted oolong, these days Ti Guan Yin leaves are rolled into loose balls (though rolled less tightly than Taiwanese high-mountain oolongs, which is why when you steep the tea, the wet leaves unroll more quickly). Until recently, most Ti Guan Yins were finished in charcoal-heated baskets to give the tea a strong baked flavor. The tea makers of Fujian have learned from Taiwanese counterparts and adopted their lighter firings. Now the best Ti Guan Yins are fired in an electric oven; as a result, the teas are much lighter and more aromatic.

OSMANTHUS

BREWING TEMPERATURE	205° to 212°F.
BREWING TIME	3–4 minutes.
DRY LEAVES	Loosely balled; a few stems evident in the dark, dull green leaves, along with occasional light orange strands of dried osmanthus blossoms.
LIQUOR	Cantaloupe orange.
AROMAS	A top note of ripe stone fruit, more apricot than peach, with the mellow spinachy flavor of green tea in the background.
BODY	The reasonably full body fills the mouth.
FLAVORS	Quite smooth, with a top note of roasted buttery carrots and apricot overlaying a vegetal green tea flavor.

Along our spectrum of oolongs, Osmanthus is the first without the floral aromas of the lighter, greener, and more "jasmonate" oolongs, the first to offer the apricot, peach, and roasted carrot flavors typical of more oxidized, darker teas. Unlike oolongs to follow, however, this one gets those flavors not from the tea, but from a flower.

A native to China, the osmanthus flower is apricot-scented with a fetching yellow orange hue. It blooms in bunches like little bouquets at the ends of its tree's branches. For centuries, the Chinese have dried the pretty flowers and used them to improve the flavors of otherwise mediocre teas. Case in point: The oolong in this tea is a lesser variety from the same region in Fujian province that makes Ti Guan Yin. While some of the tea's apricot flavors come from the tea leaves, most come from the slender strands of dried osmanthus blossoms. The pairing of the tea and blossoms is ingenious, not just as a flavor enhancer: Scientists have since shown that teas oxidized 40 percent or more, like this oolong, develop the same carotenoid aromatic compounds, called "ionones" and "damascones," that form the classic apricot and cooked peach flavors in the fruits and in the osmanthus flowers. Osmanthus is a delightful, muted dark oolong, lovely for everyday drinking.

FENGHUANG SHUIXIAN

Dragon Phoenix

BREWING TEMPERATURE	205° to 212°F.
BREWING TIME	3–4 minutes.
DRY LEAVES	Coiled leaves of a pale to earth brown with dabs of red on the edges.
LIQUOR	Pale orange.
AROMAS	The stone fruit aroma is so fresh that it almost fizzes like a Bellini of Champagne and fresh peach nectar.
BODY	Medium full, with a little astringency.
FLAVORS	Gardenia and roasted apricots.

Fenghuang ShuiXian (pronounced "Shooey-Shyan"; sometimes written as Dancong) is a worthwhile oolong to know if only because no other oolong will remind you of a Bellini. Unlike the preceding Osmanthus, which gleans much of its fruit flavors from a flower additive, Fenghuang ShuiXian bubbles with astonishing peach flavors all its own.

South of Fujian, in China's Guangdong province, the small mountain town of Fenghuang has been making teas for the city of Chaozhou for centuries. The hotter weather in the rest of southern Guangdong province is not conducive to great teas, but Fenghuang enjoys a cool mountain climate. Just as the Buddhist temples of Kyoto developed a tea culture from the green teas of the neighboring Uji region, Chaozhou has a strong Buddhist presence and a corresponding tea culture. Three Buddhist temples still stand there, as do ancient tea shops built to supply them.

Fenghuang has been making tea for centuries, and some of its tea trees could be up to five hundred years old. It's likely they were originally planted to make other kinds of tea; Chinese tea historians believe that oolong production spread to Fenghuang only after the emergence of the style in the Wuyi Mountains at the turn of the nineteenth century.

Calling these plants trees is right: Harvesters need ladders to get to the leaves. After plucking, the leaves are withered and gently tossed. This agitation starts the slow oxidation vital to form the aromatic compounds resembling peach nectar. After withering, the leaves are rolled into long twists and left to oxidize until the leaves turn light brown with red dabs on their edges. To preserve the tea's effervescence, the leaves are only lightly fired.

BAI HAO, OR
FANCIEST FORMOSA OOLONG

Oriental Beauty

BREWING TEMPERATURE	205° to 212°F.
BREWING TIME	3–4 minutes.
DRY LEAVES	Loosely balled leaves (and buds) famous for their five colors: brown, red, yellow, green, and white.
LIQUOR	Copper.
AROMAS	A wonderfully sparkly aroma with notes of tropical fruits like guava and stone fruits like peaches.
BODY	Medium.
FLAVORS	Exuberant and floral flavors of orange flower water, spring honey, fresh white peaches, and buttered toast.

This exuberant, medium-bodied Taiwanese oolong has the classic peach and guava flavors characteristic of darker, more heavily oxidized oolongs. One of the first truly great oolongs to show up in the United States about fifteen years ago, Bai Hao was also the first oolong I really fell in love with. It inspired me to hunt down all the other oolongs in the book.

Bai Hao is extraordinary not only for its flavors, but for the way it is made. Most teas rely on human manipulations to develop their flavors. These manipulations imitate the actions of tiny herbivores called green leafhoppers (*Jacobiasca formosana*), which would ordinarily feast on the leaves. In nature, the bites of tea leafhoppers trigger the plants' defenses, provoking their flavors. Bai Hao is one of only a very few teas whose flavors are provoked by the bugs themselves. Unlike the other oolongs in this book, which are all harvested in April and May, Bai Hao is harvested in June, after the leafhoppers have emerged from winter dormancy (anyone who has been bitten by a mosquito in June can understand this bug's life cycle). The leafhoppers feast on the tea's sweet young leaves, puncturing them lightly. Their munching breaks down the plants' cells in the same way rolling does, releasing various bug-repelling, flavor-filled compounds. After a week of this, the faintly perforated, fragile leafsets are nimbly harvested, with special care to keep them intact. The withered leaves—by now bug free—are gently rolled into loose, small spheres, then oxidized for a relatively long time, before being lightly fired to preserve the flavors.

DA HONG PAO
Big Red Robe

BREWING TEMPERATURE	205° to 212°F.
BREWING TIME	3–4 minutes.
DRY LEAVES	The black brown leaves have a long twist to them, resembling thick wire.
LIQUOR	Dark, clear caramel.
AROMAS	Quite smoky, but with the sweetness of stone fruits, like grilled peaches.
BODY	Medium heavy, with some astringency.
FLAVORS	Like peach compote sweetened with brown sugar or even molasses, with a similar dark edge in the finish.

This famous Chinese oolong resembles the oolongs of twenty years ago, heavily fired and with darker, smokier flavors. Fans of the smoky Chinese black tea Lapsang Souchong (page 117) or the charcoal-tinged Chinese green tea Gunpowder (page 49) will find much to love in Da Hong Pao.

Da Hong Pao grows just about an hour's drive from the area where Lapsang Souchong is cultivated in China. Both come from the Wuyi Mountains, the region in northern Fujian province where oolong and black teas were first invented. Today, a dozen or more oolongs come from the steep and rocky foothills around the city of Wuyi Shan. Known collectively as Wuyi Shan Yan Cha, or Wuyi Mountain Rock Teas, the teas take their name—and their flavors—from the area's rocky, mineral-rich soil, regular rain showers, and cool mountain weather. Unlike other high-mountain oolongs like Ali Shan (page 81), Da Hong Pao grows in the lower foothills.

While it can't claim divine inspiration like Ti Guan Yin (page 86), Da Hong Pao boasts its own rich pedigree. The stories vary, but legend says that several hundred years ago a magistrate of the Ming dynasty fell ill while visiting the area. He was nursed back to health by drinking this tea. As a token of thanks, he hung his red robe on the gate to the tea garden, granting the tea both official approbation and its name, Big Red Robe. Today, Da Hong Pao growers claim that three very old bushes outside Wuyi Shan city are the same ones that served as a coat rack for the magistrate's robe. They insist that every Da Hong Pao bush was propagated from them.

Whether or not the legend is true, the teas do provide an exquisite example of the more traditional, darker style of oolong. After the leaves are harvested, they are twisted, not balled. Unlike other twisted oolongs like Wenshan BaoZhong (page 79), Da Hong Pao is allowed to oxidize much longer. The darker tea tastes of more heavily cooked sugars and fruits like molasses and roasted peaches. Last, the tea is fired quite heavily, just as all oolongs were until very recently. Though the heavy charcoal firing has lost its usefulness as a tea preservative, Da Hong Pao drinkers prefer its taste, so the practice continues. The best teas retain their fruit flavors through the smoke.

FORMOSA OOLONG

BREWING TEMPERATURE	205° to 212°F.
BREWING TIME	3–4 minutes.
DRY LEAVES	Twisted leaves in various earth tones from dark green to dark brown, with some stems.
LIQUOR	Copper.
AROMAS	Nutty, very similar to black teas like Panyong Congou, flatter and more subdued flavor of apricots and buttered toast.
BODY	A little astringency that slightly dries the tongue.
FLAVORS	Toasted walnuts and some sweet vegetal notes of roasted carrots.

Brisk, nutty, and somewhat fruity, Formosa Oolong offers a history lesson as much as it helps cultivate your oolong palate. The tea was once considered the Champagne of teas and the standard for oolongs in the United States. In the last two decades, other lighter and more aromatic oolongs have outpaced it so that today it is made by only a handful of Taiwanese tea makers. My father included Formosa Oolong among the half dozen teas he sold when he first entered the tea business in 1970. Now we have to order it custom-made. We use it mostly as a base in our Earl Grey tea (page 171) and other blends that call for a mild, dark oolong.

In the fifteenth century when they first came upon the island, the Portuguese named Taiwan *Formosa*, or "Beautiful Island." In the tea world, Formosa and Taiwan remain interchangeable, just like Ceylon and Sri Lanka (see "Ceylon Black Teas," page 153). Formosa Oolong tea was invented in the mid-nineteenth century by a British entrepreneur named John Dodd. If they speak no other English, Taiwanese tea men can pronounce the name "John Dodd" flawlessly. They consider Dodd a national hero for first bringing the island's teas to the world stage. In 1865, Dodd saw that the world tea market was about to change dramatically. China supplied almost all the tea in the world. What Dodd knew (and the Chinese did not) was that the British were preparing, on a mass scale, to grow their own Indian tea (see "British Legacy Black Teas," page 121). Dodd shrewdly came up with a tea that he thought might compete with both the Chinese and Indian alternatives. Working in Taiwan, he developed and marketed a dark oolong under the name "Formosa Oolong." The tea traveled well yet was lighter, fruitier, and more flavorful than the heavily fired black teas then on the market. Formosa became such a hit in both Europe and the United States that it remained one of the world's favorite teas well into the twentieth century. Its popularity grew both in the United States and in Great Britain until the Japanese occupation of Taiwan all but ended production. After World War II, U.S. and British demand increased again, but after China reopened in the 1970s, demand fell off because of superior teas available from both China and Taiwan.

This tea is the only oolong in this chapter that is harvested mechanically—a process becoming increasingly common in tea as the cost of labor rises. The tea is bruised while withering to start the oxidation, twisted in a rolling machine, then left to brown to about 75 percent of the extent of pure black tea. Formosa Oolong is finished in an oven, not over charcoal, which accounts for its clean flavors. I recommend seeking this tea out, not only for its charming, gentle flavors, but also for a lesson in how quickly and thoroughly the tea world can change.

YELLOW TEAS

1. *Jun Shan Yin Zhen*

2. *Meng Ding Huang Ya*

3. *Huo Shan Huang Ya*

ellow teas offer the best of four worlds: They have the big sweet buds of white teas, the gentle vegetal flavor of green teas, the bright and changing aromas of oolongs, and the mild sweetness and soft astringent bite of the finest Chinese black teas.

The only trouble is, they are exceedingly hard to find. Yellow teas are a small but growing subset of the tea world: Only a very small quantity is made, and only a tiny portion has been available in the West (and only for the last ten years or so). The production method is a closely guarded secret. It's only a matter of time before it comes out, but until then, the few producers command top dollar for their rare, prestigious teas.

Much yellow tea on the market is fake, often simply green tea fobbed off as yellow. Genuine yellow teas, however, are hard to imitate. I have never been able to find someone who would allow me to watch them being made, so I can only speculate. I think that the leaves and buds are partially fixed to keep them only somewhat green. Since they lack the more potent aromas of oolongs and black teas, they are likely not withered. From their light yellow hue and gentle, rounded flavors, they probably oxidize very slowly and only partially, piled under thickly woven mats. To keep from masking those flavors, the leaves are likely dried in an oven, not over a fire.

The result is something extraordinary: a mesmerizing yellow gold liquor, mouth-filling body, and gentle, nuanced tropical and stone fruit flavors. What follows are three charming examples, ranging from Jun Shan Yin Zhen's soothing mango aromas to Huo Shan Huang Ya's subtle ginger flavors.

JUN SHAN YIN ZHEN
Jun Mountain Silver Needles

BREWING TEMPERATURE	175°F.
BREWING TIME	3 minutes.
DRY LEAVES	Consisting mostly of plump and downy silver green buds shaped like Yin Zhen white tea (page 21) from Fujian province, but of a more khaki or light gold color.
LIQUOR	Golden.
AROMAS	Sweet, with subtle tropical fruit notes of mango and passion fruit.
BODY	Medium.
FLAVORS	The fruit aromas don't come out much in the flavor. The light tea has the mild, sappy-sweet creaminess of panna cotta. Evocative of Yin Zhen white tea, it has more depth, nuance, and endurance.

Jun Shan Yin Zhen is one of China's finest yellow teas, with pleasing subtle fruit aromas and an enduring, balanced flavor. It comes from Jun Shan, a mountain on an island in Dongting Lake, part of the flood basin of the Yangtze River in China's Hunan province. Hunan is situated in China's interior and is usually too hot for growing tea. The lake and the mountain both provide a more moderate, cool climate in which the tea can flourish.

Plucked in the spring, the tea's sweet tips are also beloved for the way they sway vertically in a kind of dance when dropped into hot water. While at Jun Shan, I observed the Hunan version of a tea ceremony that was pleasantly less vigorous than the Japanese version. Two ladies elaborately rinsed tall glasses, filled them with hot water, and placed the leaves inside. The leaves slowly, slowly waltzed down through the water. To replicate this at home, just be sure to place the leaves on top of the water instead of pouring water over the tea.

MENG DING HUANG YA

Meng Ding Yellow Sprouts

BREWING TEMPERATURE	175°F.
BREWING TIME	3 minutes.
DRY LEAVES	Army green, slender, polished buds, largely free of down.
LIQUOR	Pale yellow green.
AROMAS	With some of the fruitiness of a very ripe mango or baked apricot and the vegetal flavor of steamed celery.
BODY	Light.
FLAVORS	Astringent but sweet vegetal flavors of fresh spring artichokes or hearts of palm.

This more astringent, slightly more vegetal yellow tea comes from Sichuan province; the Meng Ding mountain area produces most of Sichuan's better teas. Huang Ya comes from a plant different from that of Jun Shan Yin Zhen, with a slightly more developed tip. Since the tip has an external coating and less fluffy down, this tea is likely plucked later in the year than Yin Zhen as well. It has a slightly more vegetal flavor than Yin Zhen, with some light fruit notes.

HUO SHAN HUANG YA
Huo Shan Yellow Sprouts

BREWING TEMPERATURE	175°F.
BREWING TIME	3 minutes.
DRY LEAVES	Spindly, somewhat twisted buds ranging from silver yellow to dark forest green.
LIQUOR	Golden yellow.
AROMAS	Floral like a spice-scented rose; ginger and cooked fruits like canned fruit salad.
BODY	Medium light.
FLAVORS	Gingery spiciness and baked fruit, like gingered baked apricots. Very pleasant: rounded, mellow, smooth.

This gingery, floral tea is said to be an ancient tea from the Ming and Qing dynasties that was lost and rediscovered in the 1970s. But this tea is so delicious, who would lose it? It comes from the northern Anhui province. It is likely a very difficult tea to make, as its fragile bud sets are much harder to preserve than the solid buds or leaves of other yellow teas. I love its spice and apricot flavors.

CHINESE BLACK TEAS

W e've come to think of black tea as something that puckers our mouths, requiring milk and sugar to soften and soothe it. Chinese black teas, however, have all the mellow, sweetened effects of milk and sugar without requiring either. From the honeyed twinge of Golden Monkey and the Panyong teas to the chocolate of Keemuns and the turgid smokiness of Lapsang Souchong, these teas have a range and character all their own.

Given how delicious they are, it is a miracle that Chinese black teas exist. The idea that China creates black teas of this quality is as likely as the United States producing top-quality players of professional cricket. Americans play baseball. The Chinese drink green tea, and have for thousands of years. How black tea first emerged is a mystery.

Scholars believe that they first appeared at some point in the 1700s, in China's Wuyi Mountains, in northern Fujian province. It's probable that tea makers in that area had grown frustrated by the poor quality of their green teas. Looking for something to catch the attention of the Imperial Tea Tribute Board, they began to experiment with other teas that might make them some money.

Bred of the same preference for sweeter teas that has led to bud-sweetened Chinese white and green teas, Chinese black teas are loaded with glucose-laden buds. The light green buds turn gold during oxidation, the process that turns tea black. Thus many Chinese black teas have the word *Golden* in their names.

As with Chinese green teas, the buds do not give the teas a particularly pronounced sweetness. Their honeyed notes are subtler, like those of roasted carrots or even a baked but unsweetened peach. What helps amplify the dulcet quality of Chinese black teas is the way the teas darken. Generally speaking, Chinese black teas are oxidized very, very slowly, creating chemical compounds that result in a mild, soft brew that doesn't need milk to soften it.

After harvesting the tea leaves, black-tea makers do not fix their teas to preserve the green chlorophyll as green-tea makers do. Instead they allow the leaves to darken. The same reaction causes avocados and bananas to brown when their flesh is cut open and exposed to the air. During oxidation in tea, an enzyme in the leaves reacts with oxygen to create new brown-colored compounds called "flavonoids."

For more on this reaction, I encourage you to consult the more scientific appendix "From Tree to Tea" (page 193). For our tasting purposes, it's important to know that the levels of these flavonoids not only determine the tea's color, they also influence its flavors and body. As oxidation begins, the first flavonoid to emerge is called "theaflavin," which makes the tea golden but also quite brisk and puckery. If oxidation continues, milder flavonoids called "thearubigins" emerge and give the tea a rounded, gentler body and a darker brown color. The slower the oxidation, the more thearubigins, the mellower the tea.

Generally speaking, Chinese black teas consist mostly of thearubigins, since Chinese tea makers slow down oxidation as much as possible. First they roll the leaves very gently, keeping the leaves as whole as possible. Macerating the leaves only very lightly slows down oxidation by preventing the enzymes from breaking out of the leaf cells into the air. Then the tea makers pack the leaves into deep, finely woven bamboo baskets that limit access to oxygen. The leaves remain in the baskets for several hours, where they oxidize very slowly. Loaded up with thearubigins, the teas taste delightfully rounded and gentle.

Chinese black teas weren't always so sweet. Until the late 1800s, most of them were quite dark, like Keemun and Lapsang Souchong, brisker versions made for a larger British audience. Black tea was exclusively a Chinese product until the mid-nineteenth century, when the British began to grow their own tea in their colonies of India and Sri Lanka. These new tea gardens employed industrialized methods to make a remarkably brisk, uniform drink I call British Legacy Tea (see "British Legacy Black Teas," page 121). While a much diminished British market for Keemun and Lapsang did endure, the sales of Chinese black teas plummeted. The embattled Chinese sent envoys to India to learn from the new "experts," but luckily for us, the knowledge did not stick. About the only new technique the Chinese adopted from the British was the use of mechanical rolling machines (hand rolling is hard work). Unlike British Legacy Teas, which look uncannily alike (all formed on identical rolling machines, even today), Chinese teas are made using a variety of machines in myriad ways to create a panoply of shapes and flavors.

Recent innovations have made some Chinese black teas even more enticing, with the incorporation of extra buds, the same incipient leaves that give white teas their sweetness. We will start with the lightest and most modern tea, Golden

Monkey, before moving through increasingly dark teas, closing with Lapsang Souchong, one of the oldest and most famous varieties, beloved for its intensely smoky flavors.

With the exception of Lapsang Souchong, these black teas may initially seem too light. Especially to those of you who are accustomed to more robust Assams or Earl Grey, Chinese black teas may at first seem underbrewed. You're not alone. Some of my finest British hotel customers have rejected my English Breakfast blend as too weak because I make it with Chinese black teas. (There's a great saying: The British like a tea so strong, their spoon stands up in it). For those hotels, I now make a more spoon-friendly blend with brisker teas from India. That said, an open mind can be filled with new experiences. Spoon or no spoon, these Chinese teas, both ancient and more recent, can be extraordinary to sip.

GOLDEN MONKEY

BREWING TEMPERATURE	205° to 212°F.
BREWING TIME	4–5 minutes.
DRY LEAVES	Pretty twisted leaves about 1 inch long. A tippy tea, with leaves that are a mixture of about 75 percent darker brown leaves and 25 percent golden tips or buds.
LIQUOR	Pecan brown.
AROMAS	Lightly sweet: hints of apricot and nut, sometimes a mild rose aroma in the background.
BODY	Light.
FLAVORS	A blend of cooked stone fruit such as baked apricots, and the dry but slight sugariness of semisweet chocolate. A mellow, nutty finish of raw pecans.

A new tea developed for export from China in just the last ten or fifteen years, Golden Monkey has quickly attracted a loyal, almost cultlike following. With its lightly sweet, apricot aroma and hints of semisweet chocolate in the taste, it is now more popular in the United States and Europe than its older Chinese black tea cousins.

One sign of its youth is its rather innovative name. Most Chinese teas have two names, the first for the place of origin and the second for the style of leaf. Kee-mun Mao Feng, for example, is a Mao Feng style of tea from Keemun. Golden Monkey means nothing. For marketing purposes only, as "Monkey" usually does in tea names, it's meant to suggest a high-quality tea.

Golden Monkey comes from Saowu, a region outside the city of Fu'an near the coast in northern Fujian province. As with other black-tea areas in China, little green tea of any quality comes from here. The type of tea grown in the region is *Da Bai* ("big white"), a cultivar used in white tea (see "Yin Zhen," page 21). While the history is vague, it seems safe to assume that when the British export market collapsed, as in other regions, tea growers began experimenting, here first with white teas and now black.

Golden Monkey is made by a process similar to that for Panyong Congou (page 110). Tea makers harvest the leaves when the tips are as large as possible but before they have begun to form whole leaves. The tips are sweet, as they are with white teas, containing extra sugars to help the bud grow into a full leaf. However, in white teas, the bud loses its incipient chlorophyll and becomes white as the tea dries. In black tea, the same bud oxidizes to a golden color. The only trade-off: With more tips, the teas are sweeter but also lighter, with less body.

PANYONG GOLDEN NEEDLE

BREWING TEMPERATURE	205° to 212°F.
BREWING TIME	4–5 minutes.
DRY LEAVES	Flat, shiny leaves, narrow as needles, with many golden tips.
LIQUOR	Dark caramel copper.
AROMAS	Base notes of toasted walnuts with a caramelized sweetness around the edges, like fresh-baked pound cake.
BODY	Medium round.
FLAVORS	Honeylike, with a fruity top note of baked peaches and a baseline tannic quality of fresh nut skins, building to a finish of toasted walnuts.

Panyong Golden Needle, as its name suggests, has plenty of nice golden tips to make it light and sweet. As the tea has fewer tips than Golden Monkey, it also has a bit more body and more assertive fruit and nut flavors.

Panyong (also called Tanyang) is a town located in northeastern Fujian province, near Fu'an. Though the region is better known for its white teas and art teas, it has produced black teas for at least the last two hundred years. The best black teas from northern Fujian are described as tippy, for the heavy presence of golden tips. (The tips, or buds, turn from white to gold during oxidation.) Unlike the coiled, floral Golden Monkey, Panyong Golden Needle has straight, needlelike leaves with nuttier flavors but similar fruity charms. The flat leaves can have a pleasant sheen to them: They are polished in a slightly heated wok, rubbed up against the metal surface repeatedly to polish them. Unlike the more heavily fired black teas from the Wuyi Shan region, Panyong teas are finished in an oven. Discerning tea makers do not like fire flavors to overpower these rounded teas.

PANYONG CONGOU

BREWING TEMPERATURE	205° to 212°F.
BREWING TIME	4–5 minutes.
DRY LEAVES	Small, dark brown matte curls, with just a few golden buds blended in.
LIQUOR	Raw sienna.
AROMAS	Nutty, with only a faint edge of honeyed sweetness.
BODY	Medium full.
FLAVORS	Soft and lovely, unabrasive flavors of baked but unsweetened apples and some spring hay.

Continuing our progression from light and sweet to dark and smoky, we have Panyong Congou, which exhibits fewer honey notes but greater heft than the previous two teas. Those who prefer full-bodied British Legacy Teas will find much to like in Panyong Congou. From the same area in Fujian province, Pan-yong Congou is a close relative of Panyong Golden Needle and Golden Monkey but slightly older and made in a more traditional style, with the least amount of tips. *Congou* is a corruption of the Chinese words *Gong Fu,* or *Kung Fu,* which mean "Highest Mastery." A tea trade classification for Chinese black teas with this particular twisted shape, the word refers to the masterful skill required to produce the teas by hand. Today, the teas are made almost entirely by machine. The leaves are expertly rolled into a tight twist before slowly oxidizing to take on the fruity but unsweetened flavors of baked apples.

KEEMUN MAO FENG
Keemun Downy Tip

BREWING TEMPERATURE	205° to 212°F.
BREWING TIME	3–4 minutes.
DRY LEAVES	Long, skinny leaves, many of which end in golden tips. The leaves are slightly twisted.
LIQUOR	Pale orange brown.
AROMAS	Light notes of chocolate or cocoa with the suggestion of ripe apricots.
BODY	Medium light.
FLAVORS	Light and sweet, with hints of chocolate and the stone fruit flavors of baked apricots. Top floral flavors of roses.

Arguably China's most famous black tea, Keemun Mao Feng has been a Western favorite for over a century. Darker than Panyong Congou, both Keemun Mao Feng and Keemun Hao Ya A, following, are famous for their intriguing chocolate flavors. Keemuns have a captivating quality that evokes unsweetened cocoa, but without the bitterness.

The name *Keemun* is an older Western spelling of the town now known as Qimen (pronounced "Chee-men"). The tea grows near the town, in a region between the Yellow Mountains and the Yangtze River. The rolling flats can get quite steep. The little hills are stumpy compared with the dramatic peaks of Darjeeling and a far cry from the terraced hills of Wuyi, where Lapsang Souchong comes from. The green teas grown in Qimen (as in every other black-tea region in China) are second-rate, hence the region's interest in making black tea for export.

Mao Feng is a more elegant, lighter, and more refined Keemun than its cousin Hao Ya A. This sophistication is due in part to the earlier harvest; Mao Feng is gathered over just a few days in late April and early May, earlier in the spring when the leaves contain softer, rounder polyphenols and superior amino acids. Mao Feng is also harvested in leafsets of two leaves and a bud, whereas Hao Ya A contains mostly full leaves. Buds lighten and sweeten Mao Feng. I recommend tasting both Keemuns together to compare.

Both teas undergo an unusually long wither of between three and four hours, which makes the teas more aromatic. After withering, the tea is rolled and slowly oxidized for around five hours, almost twice as long as many British Legacy Teas. Then the leaves are gently yet thoroughly rolled. The rolling machines give the leaves a lovely twist. The rolling also accentuates the buds to make them look larger than they are. After the rolling, the leaves are loaded into long, deep bamboo baskets and covered with cloth. The baskets stand in a steam-filled room. Over the hours, the tips turn a charming golden color and the leaves begin to acquire the cocoa flavors for which Keemuns are so famous.

Keemun Mao Feng is quite rare. Most Keemun tea makers skip the Mao Feng harvest, saving their leaves for the Hao Ya harvest that begins just a few days later and lasts much longer. Fruitier and lighter than its later-season cousin, Keemun Mao Feng remains a treat worth trying.

KEEMUN HAO YA A

BREWING TEMPERATURE	205° to 212°F.
BREWING TIME	4–5 minutes.
DRY LEAVES	A mixture of dark leaves and golden buds, but less tippy and with shorter and thicker leaves than Keemun Mao Feng.
LIQUOR	Dark copper.
AROMAS	Redolent of chocolate, darker, and with a more intense roasted aroma than Keemun Mao Feng.
BODY	Medium—more body and more intensity than Keemun Mao Feng, with a little astringency.
FLAVORS	Darker and more chocolaty than Mao Feng, with fewer fruit or floral notes.

As I've discussed in the previous section on Keemun Mao Feng, Keemuns are some of China's oldest and most renowned black teas. They come from the rolling hills surrounding the small town now written as *Qimen*. The tea fields lie between the Yellow Mountains and the Yangtze River. Hao Ya is made in late April or early May, after the Mao Feng harvest, when the leaves are bigger and more flavorful. While Mao Feng is harvested over only eight to ten days, Hao Ya season goes on for as long as six weeks.

Ha Ya teas are separated: The best tips become Ha Ya A, the next-best tips become Ha Ya B. The grading system is an affectation adopted for the U.S. market; A and B grades don't exist in China.

Hao Ya A is processed much like Keemun Mao Feng. Whereas Mao Feng makers accentuate the bud, drawing out the subtlety and sweetness of the tea, Hao Ya makers go for power. When buying Ha Ya A, I look for the enduring intensity that is characteristic of the very best Ha Ya A teas.

YUNNAN BLACK TEA

BREWING TEMPERATURE	205° to 212°F.
BREWING TIME	4–5 minutes.
DRY LEAVES	Slightly twisted inch-long leaves, a mixture of dark black leaves and golden tips, all covered by the faintest film of golden down.
LIQUOR	Dark caramel.
AROMAS	An earthiness characteristic of most Yunnan teas, with some sweetness, edging toward maple syrup.
BODY	Medium bold; somewhat astringent.
FLAVORS	Matching the aromas, earthy with an edge of maple sweetness.

If Keemuns are the aristocrats of Chinese black teas, Yunnan black teas are the poor but happy cousins. Earthy, almost gutty and assertive, the teas also have a sociable maple sweetness to give them accessible charm. This sugared note makes for an instructive contrast to the sophisticated, subdued chocolate flavors of Keemuns. The maple and chocolate notes are both products of the Maillard reaction that occurs during firing, when amino acids and glucosides in the leaves combine to form compounds called "pyrroles" and "pyrazines," chemicals that have sweet roasted flavors. Yunnan and Keemun leaves have different levels of amino acids; those in Yunnan form pyrazines that remind me of cooked maple sap.

Yunnan black tea comes from a remote region of China on the border of Laos and Burma, where tea is thought to have originated. Most teas from this region are aged to make puerhs (page 173). Puerhs have become so popular, it is getting harder and harder to find unaged ordinary Yunnan black tea. But it is worth searching out. Yunnan black tea offers a delicious combination of full body and sweetish flavors, with a certain earthiness and even a mild pepperiness, balanced by the sugars from lots of tip. There is even a 100 percent golden tip tea made in Yunnan, called Dianhong. Teas made entirely of tips are so expensive, I wanted to include only one in the book. Because I find Dianhong inferior, I've chosen Golden Tip Assam (page 144).

LAPSANG SOUCHONG

BREWING TEMPERATURE	205° to 212°F.
BREWING TIME	4–5 minutes.
DRY LEAVES	Small, a dull jet black, with no golden tips. Lesser versions have larger leaves.
LIQUOR	Orange brown caramel color. The smokier the tea, the darker the liquor.
AROMAS	Good Lapsangs have a remarkably powerful, lovely, sweet, smoked aroma. A mixture of pine and hardwood smoke, fruit, and spice, with faint hints of orange spiked with cloves. Smokier varieties veer toward stronger, meatier smells of beef or bacon. In lesser grades, the sweetness disappears in place of an incredibly strong smell of tar.
BODY	Medium heavy.
FLAVORS	The flavor usually matches the aromas: pine smoke and dark stone fruit; sometimes bacony and meaty with a very long finish.

With a captivating smoky flavor unlike any other tea—black, green, or otherwise—Lapsang Souchong is the oldest and among the most beloved of all the black teas from China. When I first started in the tea business with my father in the mid-1980s, Lapsang Souchong was one of the half dozen teas we sold. Today we sell over three hundred teas, but Lapsang remains a favorite. It's been sold in the United States for two hundred years.

There are countless varieties of Lapsang Souchong. Lesser varieties are generally more acrid and more intense, while the finest are lighter and more refined. Though teas marketed as Lapsang Souchong now come from all over the world, the true version still comes from the spot considered to be the birthplace of black tea, China's Wuyi Mountains, in the northern part of Fujian province. No one knows why or how black teas started there; as with the other black teas in this chapter, it probably had something to do with the fact that the green teas grown there weren't that great. I rarely find green teas in the Wuyi region, only black teas and oolongs. Even the oolongs, called Wuyi Mountain Rock Teas, are among the darker varieties (see "Da Hong Pao," page 93).

The Wuyi Preserve is breathtaking. Surrounded by a stark forest of dark pine and light bamboo, the road to the tea-growing regions rises through a narrowing canyon along a raging stream. Inside this chasm, tea plants are naturally protected: The special cultivar that grows here is prevented from breeding with any other. The plants grow low to the ground and are allowed to spread on their own, untreated with chemicals or fertilizers. As a result, harvesting from the rambling, low bushes is tough work.

Until only a few years ago, the production method for Lapsang Souchong was a closely guarded secret. As the Chinese government devolves control of its tea factories back to private citizens, however, access to this information has improved, as have the teas themselves.

Lapsang Souchong leaves are infused with their smoke flavors in two stages. Once they are harvested, the leaves are withered for two hours to make them supple, in a room above a chamber where an even fire of native pine logs slowly smolders.

After withering, the leaves are rolled to form small, spindly needles. The rolling starts the oxidation. The oxidizing needles are loaded up in tall woven bamboo baskets and covered with a cloth. Gathered together in deep baskets and covered from the open air, the leaves take on the much more gentle flavors characteristic of Chinese black teas. Unlike Keemuns, the teas oxidize in a dry room free from steam, and have no trace of chocolate flavor.

After two hours of oxidizing, the dark brown leaves are spread out on bamboo trays and moved to a small room above the same smoking chamber where the leaves are withered. The same hot, piney smoke rises from the level below. The leaves rest there for four hours, drying out and absorbing a smoky flavor like so many tiny slabs of bacon. When they are finished, the scent of dried Lapsang leaves is as much a pleasure to savor as the actual taste of the tea.

BRITISH LEGACY BLACK TEAS

It's common to presume that Darjeeling, Assam, and Ceylon teas have as much ancient history as do Keemun, Lung Ching, Sencha, and the other great teas of China and Japan. While teas from South Asia are also incredible, they are, remarkably, only a little older than the telegraph. Named for the regions where they grow, these teas are a product of the British Empire, when British industrialists first established tea plantations in their then colonies. In the last fifty years, since the region won its independence from Great Britain, the tea styles, too, have evolved. Native tea makers have found ways to give them more nuance and character than the original industrial combines first sought. All three styles of tea retain some marks of British influence, so I group them together under my own term, British Legacy Teas.

Historically, these British Legacy Teas were both revered and derided for assertive, unsubtle flavors and brisk, tannic body. These are the teas that made black tea famous for its pucker. Today, many of the teas have evolved to become considerably more sophisticated. They retain some of that characteristic British Legacy bite but now boast nuance, charms, and engaging flavors ranging from guava to dark honey and malt.

British Legacy Teas were originally developed to require the mellowing effects of milk and sugar. By the 1830s, when Samuel Morse first started tinkering with wires, the British Empire was nearing its apogee. Tea consumption was rapidly increasing with the prosperity born of the Industrial Revolution. A new class of factory workers depended on tea with sugar and milk to supply them with a surprisingly large portion of their nutrition. Paying China for all that tea, however, was causing severe cash shortages. The British began looking for ways to get tea for free. Numerous attempts were made to establish tea plantations in the new colony of India.

After much trial and error, by the 1850s the British had succeeded. They found that *Camellia sinensis* var. *sinensis,* the native Chinese variety of the tea plant, thrived in the cool, steep mountain slopes of northeastern India's Darjeeling region. In the nearby province of Assam, botanists discovered an entirely separate variety of tea plant, a larger-leafed variety they called *Camellia sinensis* var. *assamica*. Vast plantations quickly grew up in that flatter and more low-lying region, churning out immense quantities of *assamica's* larger leaves. In the 1870s, Scots brought both varieties of tea to Sri Lanka, or what was then called Ceylon, after a blight wiped out coffee crops there.

In all three places, the British appetite for cheap tea led the new British tea merchants to reinvent the beverage. At first, the British tried to imitate the Chinese style of tea making. However, they soon found that their new vast tropical tea farms rendered the Chinese methods impracticable. These new estates produced tea in quantities never seen before in either China or Japan. The hot climate pushed out leaves year-round—quite large leaves in the case of the *assamica* plant—more leaves than human hands could shape or fire over woks. What's more, in the time Chinese tea makers allowed their leaves to wither, South Asian tea leaves would rot in the climate's heat and humidity. The British applied their industrial innovations to tea making, combining steps or cutting them out altogether, introducing machinery to tackle what had for so long been done by hand. In the process, they created a new type of tea.

INDIA · SRI LANKA

—— India/Sri Lanka Boundary ★ National Capital

- - - International Boundary ◉ State or Union Territory Capital

—— River

⛰ Mountain Range • City or Town

© 2008 Meighan Cavanaugh

NEW DELHI

DARJEELING

Brahmaputra River

ASSAM

India

CALCUTTA

BOMBAY

Arabian Sea

Bay of Bengal

NILGIRI MOUNTAINS

Sri Lanka (Ceylon)

KENILWORTH

COLOMBO

Uva Highlands

New Vithanakande

← *Kenya*

Indian Ocean

The British invented heated withering tables to speed up the evaporation necessary to soften tea leaves for rolling. They invented the very first rolling machines, one aptly called the Britannia. The machine is still in use in many Indian tea gardens today. These rolling machines precipitated the need for a new grading system. Chinese black teas had always consisted of whole leaves, but these new mechanical rollers generated all manner of leaf particles, leading to new variations in the brew. To distinguish one from another, British Legacy Teas, particularly those from the Indian tea regions of Darjeeling and Assam, still come with a string of letters and numbers attached to their names explaining their leaf size. These terms are so common, it's worth attempting to define them. Let's look at the tail on a typical top-quality Indian variety:

S: Special
F: Fancy
T: Tippy
G: Golden
F: Flowery / B: Broken
O: Orange
P: Pekoe
1: Number 1

As you can see, the region suffers from grade inflation. Only forty years ago, the best British Legacy Teas were labeled GFOP or BOP, for Golden Flowery Orange Pekoe and Broken Orange Pekoe, respectively. Increased competition over a shrinking market has led tea makers to tack on ever more modifiers in a misguided effort to stand out. *Supreme, Special, Fancy, Tippy, Number 1, Golden,* and *Orange Pekoe* are all meant to suggest little more than best-quality teas. Orange Pekoe is nearly meaningless; "Orange" stands for the Dutch Royal

House of Orange and once indicated tea of a quality suitable for their monarchs. "Pekoe" is a mispronunciation of the Chinese words *bai hao*—*bai* meaning "white" and *hao* meaning "tippy" or "downy." *Pekoe* may have once meant tippy teas, but the ancient word has long since lost its original meaning.

The two words to look for are *Flowery* or *Broken*. *Flowery* meant tippy in the era when British tea makers thought that the buds came from the flowers of the tea bush, before they realized the buds were incipient leaves. Today, Flowery mostly means a tea made up of the largest available particles. *Broken* means the tea consists of smaller, broken pieces. Generally speaking, the larger the leaf particles, the mellower and more sophisticated the tea.

Today, both Flowery and Broken teas are also called "Orthodox" teas, to distinguish them from "CTC" teas. "CTC" teas (so called for the "Crush, Tear, and Curl" steps of the production process) were introduced into the market in 1931, when Sir William McKercher invented the a machine that would "crush, tear, and curl" the fresh tea leaves in one fell swoop. This technique, the apogee of British tea innovation, revolutionized the world of tea production. Essentially a massive sieve, the machine extruded fresh leaves as tiny bright green pellets, then sent them on a conveyor belt beneath powerful blowers. This machine so hastened oxidation that the pellets turned dark brown within one hundred yards, in just under an hour. The result of this near instantaneous oxidation was a tea with extraordinary briskness and consistency. CTC teas have much less of the sort of internal variation that pure whole-leaf teas can provide, the kind of magical alteration that happens when one sips a fine tea or wine. CTC teas are so much cheaper and easier to produce, however, that they have almost entirely supplanted Orthodox teas. Today, CTC teas make up at least 95 percent of the worldwide tea market and are the primary ingredient in teabags. But because they are so blunt, I include only one CTC in this book. All the other British Legacy Teas here are Orthodox, and of those, almost all are Flowery.

In the British Legacy areas, the market for both Orthodox and CTC British Legacy Teas began to shrink dramatically in 1947 when the British Raj ended. The British began importing the bulk of their black tea from East Africa. South Asians took over ownership of the plantations, and British influence in the region waned. The makers of the best Darjeelings, Assams, and Ceylons began innovating to appeal to a broader reach of tea drinkers. In the last thirty to forty years, many have taken advantage of modernizations in production and tea transport to improve their teas. The best Orthodox Darjeelings now have bright fruity qualities to rival oolongs. Honeyed, malty Assams have won a loyal following for their assertive, robust flavors. Ceylons are winning notice for creativity and invention, seemingly producing a new and different style for each garden on the small island. It is these more recent—and more delicious—teas that we will taste now.

DARJEELING BLACK TEAS

1. *Singbulli SFTGFOP1 Supreme Dj 18*

2. *Margaret's Hope FTGFOP Muscatel Dj 275*

3. *Himalayan Tips SFTGFOP1 Second Flush*

4. *Okayti Dj 480 Autumnal FTGFOP*

The northeastern region of Darjeeling on the border of Nepal and Bhutan is famous for three seasons of tea: the spring's First Flush, the early summer's Second Flush, and the late summer and fall's Autumnal teas. Though they grow more subdued the farther they get from spring, all three seasonal teas have a charming rounded quality, a depth and a gentleness to rival Chinese black teas. The First Flushes in particular have lively floral and fruit aromas to rival oolongs. We will try all of them.

I place Darjeelings first in this unit on British Legacy Teas not only because they were the first teas made by the Raj, but also because they most closely resemble Chinese black teas and are the most natural progression to follow them. Crafted to give a similar rounded quality, Darjeelings also have more tropical fruit flavors like pineapple and guava, and a little more bite than Chinese Black teas from their more hastened oxidation.

Darjeeling has produced teas only since the 1830s. In their quest to grow tea in India, the British discovered that the native Chinese tea bush, *Camellia sinensis* var. *sinensis,* flourished there. In what remains one of the highest-altitude tea-growing regions in the world, in the cool air and hardscrabble soil of the Himalayan foothills, the tea leaves grow slowly, taking on lovely variegated flavors. Though British plantations marketed their product as the Champagne of teas, what they churned out was heavy, dark, and brisk, almost begging for the softening effects of milk and sugar. I still have older customers who pine for this traditional Darjeeling flavor.

In 1947, independence brought an end to the Raj, and British influence in the region waned. Great Britain began importing the bulk of its teas from Africa. In the late 1960s, in a search for new teas to capture a fresh audience, Bernd Wulf, founder of HTH, the tea wholesaling firm my family buys from, worked with an Indian tea dealer named Ranabir Sen. The two experimented with lightening the teas to let the leaves' flavorful qualities come through.

First they made sure that the harvesters gathered only the most flavorful parts of the plant. Following the Chinese example, the harvesters snipped only young leafsets of two leaves and a bud. Then they lengthened the withering time to build up the teas' extraordinary aromas and give them a lighter, almost greenish cast. You'll recall that oolong tea makers wither tea leaves right after harvesting them to soften them up for rolling. In Darjeeling, to fight off the cold and damp weather, tea makers wither their leaves in heated troughs. Wulf and Sen found that if they left the leaves in the troughs long after the leaves had gone limp, in what's now called a "hard wither," the teas took on remarkably strong aromas similar to those of oolongs. The tea's flavors also became more complex. Hard withering kept many of the leaves green by deactivating a percentage of the enzyme that would otherwise turn the green leaves brown. The hard withering affects different cultivars to varying degrees; since most gardens use a variety of clones, many good Darjeelings have a beautiful mixture of black and green leaves.

Wulf and Sen also carefully adjusted the rolling process, making sure the teas did not get overheated and lose their flavors from excess pressure or friction. They monitored the oxidation and shortened the firing time significantly, to show off the improvements in flavor rather than cover them with a heavy firing.

Thanks to their efforts, today we can enjoy a range of aromatic, flavorful Darjeeling teas. We will begin with a bright and floral First Flush Darjeeling. Then we'll taste a great, though more subdued, Second Flush. We'll end with two teas with characteristic mellow but assertive Autumnal Darjeeling flavors.

Since Darjeelings are more delicate than Assams, they are best brewed at lower temperatures, between 190 and 212 degrees Fahrenheit, and for only three to four minutes. Experiment to see what works best. In general, the later the tea is harvested in the season, the higher the water temperature should be.

SINGBULLI SFTGFOP1 SUPREME DJ 18

Singbulli Special Fancy Tippy Golden Flowery Orange Pekoe No. 1

BREWING TEMPERATURE	190° to 212°F.
BREWING TIME	3–4 minutes.
DRY LEAVES	A lovely mixture of silver tips and burnt sienna, sage, and forest green leaves, surprisingly light in color for a black tea. The leaves are twisted, but haphazardly so, unlike the careful, deliberate twists of Chinese black teas.
LIQUOR	Yellow brown, the color of passion fruit.
AROMAS	So aromatic, it almost qualifies as a minor oolong. Hints of ginger and cardamom, along with a subtle citrus note suggestive of the freshly torn rind of a ruby red grapefruit.
BODY	Medium; brisker than most Chinese teas, filling the mouth with sensation, but not offputtingly puckery like some lesser Darjeelings.
FLAVORS	Lively, with suggestions of bright fruit flavors like pineapple and grapefruit.

Singbulli is one of Darjeeling's better gardens, stretching over the foothills of the Himalayas at the base of Kangchenjunga, the third highest peak in the world. Although some distance from the city of Darjeeling, Singbulli is still part of the Darjeeling region. The road to the garden offers one of the most scenic drives in all of tea country: It loops through tea fields, following the crests of the hills before plunging into the tea-carpeted Mirik Valley. While much of Darjeeling teas suffer from an overuse of modifiers, Singbulli teas really are supreme. With its spicy, lively aromas, its bracing body, fruity flavors, and colorful green and brown leaves, the tea is a model First Flush Darjeeling.

Like Chinese Qing Ming teas and Japanese Senchas, First Flush Darjeelings consist of the first leaves and buds to flush in early spring. Spring teas are so prized because they have a bigger share of what makes tea so delicious. During the winter the plants go dormant, storing sugars and other compounds in their roots. As the weather warms, the plants send out those sugars and other tasty compounds to the tips of the plants to fuel new leaf growth. In the cool spring weather, the leaves grow slowly, making their flavor compounds even more concentrated and complex.

To help bring out these more nuanced flavors, Singbulli tea makers oxidize First Flush teas for less time than they do teas harvested later in the season. They stop the First Flush after what they call "the first nose," a particular scent that emerges about two hours after the leaves are rolled. First Flush teas are therefore quite green, both because of their shorter oxidation and because of hard withering.

In the last ten years, competition over the earliest First Flush teas has gotten quite intense. Few people in India take any notice of them, since the national beverage there is *chai* from CTC teas. Nonetheless, tea drinkers in Germany and, increasingly, Japan and the United States are quite fond of them. First Flush teas are flown into Japan like Beaujolais Nouveau is; some Japanese tea shops even display signs that read, "The First Flush has arrived." Japanese businessmen increasingly offer Darjeeling First Flush teas to colleagues as tokens of respect.

Though they may be prestigious, the very first teas of the First Flush season are usually a little thin. Unlike Qing Ming teas and Senchas, First Flush teas actually peak a few weeks into the harvest. While tea buyers compete over the very first lots of the season, it's actually better to wait to see which lots are the best.

Singbulli's First Flush season starts around the second week of March and lasts roughly three weeks. The Dj 18 in this tea's name indicates that the tea was harvested about two weeks into the harvest, the eighteenth lot to be picked.

MARGARET'S HOPE FTGFOP MUSCATEL DJ 275

Margaret's Hope Fancy Tippy Golden Flowery Orange Pekoe Muscatel Darjeeling Lot No. 275

BREWING TEMPERATURE	190° to 212°F.
BREWING TIME	4–5 minutes.
DRY LEAVES	The exact same shape as every other tea in this chapter, a mixture of leaf sizes, some whole but most broken, all shaped by the same Britannia rolling machine. The leaves are a charming mixture of browns—burnt sienna, sienna, and pale yellow white buds.
LIQUOR	Dull copper.
AROMAS	Cooked stone fruit flavors like dried dates, poached apricots, or baked peaches and hints of spice. Reminiscent of Muscat grapes, hence the label Muscatel.
BODY	Medium, with some astringency.
FLAVORS	Rounded and mellow, with the similar stone fruit flavors of apricots and peaches.

Margaret's Hope contains all the mellow, more subdued, cooked stone fruit character of a classic Second Flush Darjeeling. This is also called a Muscatel Darjeeling, since its flavor is suggestive of Muscat grapes.

Second Flush teas are to First Flush teas a little like what Banchas are to Senchas in Japan; like Banchas, Second Flush leaves emerge a few weeks after the First Flush passes. The First Flush lasts for three to four weeks in early spring, ending when the plant has spent all its stored winter energy on new leaves. For several weeks, the plant does not make any leaves as it regenerates energy. Then in late May or early June, the plant starts to grow again. Though bigger and tougher than the tender First Flush leaves, Second Flush leaves are still full of flavor.

Darjeeling tea makers adjust their production methods from First Flush to Second Flush to accommodate the larger, older leaves. As Taiwanese tea makers do with Bai Hao, also called the Fanciest Formosa Oolong (page 91), Darjeeling tea makers harness the plants' self-defenses by allowing their natural predators, leaf mites, to feast on the leaves right before harvesting them. During the feasting, the leaves repel the predators by releasing defenses in the form of aromatic compounds. When the tea is made, the compounds create the lovely fruity flavors.

As with First Flush teas, the tea makers hard-wither the leaves after harvesting to concentrate their aromas. After rolling the leaves, they oxidize them 30 percent longer. First Flush teas oxidize until the first nose—a certain distinctive, strong aroma that emerges after about two hours. Second Flush teas oxidize for about another forty minutes to an hour. The first nose dies away after ten minutes; after another thirty minutes or so, the second nose emerges, at which point the tea maker fires the leaves in an oven. The firing lasts just under half an hour, to add gentle roasted flavors.

HIMALAYAN TIPS SFTGFOP1 SECOND FLUSH

Himalayan Tips Special Fancy Tippy Golden Flowery Orange Pekoe No. 1 Second Flush

BREWING TEMPERATURE	190° to 212°F.
BREWING TIME	4–5 minutes.
DRY LEAVES	Thick, brown green leaves with a few silver tips mixed in.
LIQUOR	Light copper caramel.
AROMAS	A tropical fruit aroma like guava or passion fruit, along with a pronounced honey aroma.
BODY	Medium full; quite astringent, though still rounded.
FLAVORS	The tropical fruit notes are not as assertive as in the aromas. The honey is there, but without the polish of the scent.

This tea comes from Nepal. While not technically a Darjeeling, it is made in the Darjeeling style, with a hard wither, thorough rolling, limited oxidation, and light firing. Darjeeling teas are made right on the border separating India from Nepal, so it is only natural that tea cultivation has migrated to the other side of the border. Nepalese teas were once marketed as Darjeelings, but Himalayan Tips is proudly sold as tea from Nepal.

Himalayan Tips comes from a promising new garden started just a few years ago called Jun Chiyabari. A small operation about thirty miles west of the border, Jun Chiyabari supplements its own leaf production with leaves from other local Nepalese tea farmers. In coming years, the garden's teas should only get better, but for now its finest tea, a Second Flush, lacks the nuance and full range of flavor of Margaret's Hope. The tea still serves as a useful indicator of the rising quality of Nepalese teas.

OKAYTI DJ 480 AUTUMNAL FTGFOP

Okayti Darjeeling Lot No. 480 Autumnal Fancy Tippy Golden Flowery Orange Pekoe

BREWING TEMPERATURE	190° to 212°F.
BREWING TIME	4–5 minutes.
DRY LEAVES	A mixture of brown and green leaves of many different sizes and, unfortunately, stalk.
LIQUOR	Light caramel.
AROMAS	Faint roasted flavors of toasted macadamia nuts; some ginger spiciness and tropical fruit notes evoking passion fruit and pineapple.
BODY	Medium-bodied with a gentle bite.
FLAVORS	Higher-pitched tropical fruit flavors of passion fruit and pineapple, without the stone fruit flavors of other black teas. More subdued than the aromas.

Okayti possesses the classic qualities of Autumnal Darjeeling: mildly fruity and spicy—and affordable. The third style of Darjeelings, Autumnal teas are harvested after the late-summer monsoon, an event unique to the teas of South Asia. The monsoon hits Darjeeling around the end of June (depending on the valley and the elevation), drawing a close to the Second Flush season. Sometime around October, when the clouds clear and good tea weather recommences, the Autumnal tea harvest begins.

The Dj 480 portion of Okayti's name indicates that the tea is a Darjeeling from the 480th lot of that plantation to be harvested that year, most likely in November. The garden of Okayti stands on the lower hills of the Darjeeling region abutting Nepal. Although a perfectly good garden, it generally does not produce teas at the level of Margaret's Hope or Singbulli. Autumnal teas are made much like Second Flush teas; the thicker leaves are left to oxidize through the second nose, or for about three hours, before being fired to take on mild roasted flavors. The result is a muted version of a Second Flush.

Okayti is a nostalgic favorite of mine. Situated on a lovely corner of a road through the Mirik Valley, it is a stunningly beautiful garden. When my mentor, Bernd Wulf, died, his ashes were scattered here. Whenever we are in the area, a visit is mandatory.

Queen Victoria also found teas from this garden enjoyable. Legend credits her for the name: After trying it, she pronounced that it was indeed "okay tea."

NILGIRI BLACK TEAS

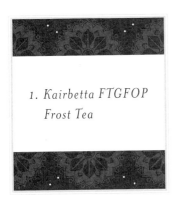

1. Kairbetta FTGFOP Frost Tea

N ilgiri means "Blue Mountain"; part of the Western Ghats mountain range in southern India, the Nilgiris are also the most scenic tea region in India—which is saying a lot, considering Darjeeling's stunning mountain scenery and the enchanting tea carpet of Assam. Found in Tamil Nadu, bordering Kerala, the Nilgiris combine beautiful mountains with an abundance of blooming flowers. The British established the first tea plantation here in 1854. After experiencing the heat of the plains, I can understand the attraction of the cooler highlands where the tea is grown. The region grew to become a major producer with several hundred tea estates. After India's independence, the Nilgiris became a volume producer of CTC teas rather than a source of quality Orthodox teas. Unfortunately, this trend predominates today, which is why this section is so short. Kairbetta is a tea made in the cold months of December and January. Its aromas are delightful enough that I thought the tea merited its own section.

KAIRBETTA FTGFOP FROST TEA

Kairbetta Fancy Tippy Golden Flowery Orange Pekoe Frost Tea

BREWING TEMPERATURE	212°F.
BREWING TIME	5 minutes.
DRY LEAVES	Long, twisted gray-brown leaves with some silver tips.
LIQUOR	Russet brown.
AROMAS	Guava and some orange blossom citrus notes. Quite lively in the nose.
BODY	Medium light.
FLAVORS	Not as strong as the aroma, with similar fruity grain flavors, but mere hints of the floral tones.

Kairbetta is a garden located in southern India, in the tea district called the Nilgiris ("Blue Mountains"). Kairbetta is called a "frost tea" because it is made during the cold, dry months from December to February. In the southern Indian winter, the tea plants do not go dormant, but the leaves do grow more slowly, concentrating the tea's aromatic compounds. The cold weather also allows the factories to wither and oxidize the teas more slowly as well, further developing the aroma compounds to draw out their attractive fruit, floral, and spice notes. With its lovely aromas but dark color, Kairbetta falls somewhere between a First Flush and Second Flush Darjeeling.

ASSAM BLACK TEAS

1. *Golden Tip Assam*

2. *Mangalam FTGFOP OR 815*

3. *Mangalam FTGBOP Special OR 555*

4. *Boisahabi CTC PF 642*

The twirling brown leaves and golden tips of the world's greatest Assam black teas yield lovely honey and malty flavors, a little like the maltiness of a good beer. Assams are also among the most assertive and brisk of the black teas. It's no accident: The more quickly a tea is made, the brisker its body. And everything about Assam tea is fast.

Assam is India's tea basket, a hothouse region that generates astonishing quantities of tea in just six weeks. Assam teas derive from *Camellia sinensis* var. *assamica,* a large-leafed variety of tea discovered only in the 1830s by British botanist-adventurer Charles Bruce. As in Darjeeling, the British were quick to establish massive tea plantations, which today grow many different clones of the wild original. (Assam also has a very large field of natural gas, so in an awkward—though safe—arrangement, today the tea plantations alternate with gas refineries.)

In Assam's subtropical conditions, the plants suffer for nothing, least of all water: Assam is one of the wettest places on the planet. The mighty Brahmaputra River cuts right down the Y-shaped northeastern region, brimming with melted Himalayan snows and the region's rains. The weather is fairly consistent: It either pours down rain or it is sunny and steamy. In the tropical moisture, the tea bushes draw from the rich, alluvial soil to generate thick, big leaves from May through June. In the humid air, tea makers have to rush to process the tea.

Assam makers both wither and oxidize these leaves in less time than for just about every other good tea. In contrast with oolong leaves, which benefit from multistage withering, or Darjeelings, which require a hard withering, Assam leaves are limp and ready for rolling after just eighteen hours. As a result of this soft wither, Assams are more muted, more soothing, and a darker, richer brown color.

Assam makers roll and oxidize their teas quickly as well. While most use CTC machines, a few great Orthodox Assam makers apply traditional rolling to macerate the large, thick *assamica* leaves. First they roll the leaves in large batches in strong machines that apply plenty of pneumatic pressure. The leaf morsels that are the first to break down are considered the best and are called "fines" (see "Mangalam FTGFOP OR 815," page 146). The remaining leaves are run through a conical sieve called a "*dhool.*" This sieve pulverizes the leaves much as a ricer does a potato. Some leaves are still too tough and are sent through the rolling machine and then the *dhool* a second and third time. The thoroughly crushed leaves then oxidize very quickly, taking on strong, brisk flavors.

Orthodox Assams are the finest of the region, but they are risky to make. Indians drink primarily CTC tea, most often as *chai,* intoxicating with spices and hot milk. But as a result, the domestic market for whole-leaf, Orthodox Assams is tiny. The best Orthodox Assams come from large industrial gardens that can afford to take a chance. Belying the usual assumptions about artisanal teas, some of Assam's finest Orthodox teas come from enormous multinational corporations. The two Mangalams in this chapter come from Jayshree Tea & Industries, a publicly traded company listed on the Bombay Stock Exchange with a market capitalization of over $50 million.

These companies have helped improve the quality of the region's teas dramatically in the last fifty years. Though Assams have changed considerably, I have a nostalgic affection for them. I start my day with an Assam. Of the pure teas I trade in, Assams most resemble the dark black teas of my childhood. Only today they taste so much better.

What follows are four Assams, arranged in order from most honeyed to guttiest and most robust. The first, Golden Tip Assam, is a recent innovation, as the name suggests, made entirely of golden tips. The next two Mangalams represent more traditional, robust Orthodox teas. The fourth is a top-notch (though strong and uniform) CTC.

GOLDEN TIP ASSAM

BREWING TEMPERATURE	190° to 212°F.
BREWING TIME	4–5 minutes.
DRY LEAVES	All golden tips, each about ½ inch long. The tips are coated in fine, golden, downy powder.
LIQUOR	Reddish peach.
AROMAS	Light honey and malt aromas.
BODY	Full-bodied.
FLAVORS	Caramel-buttery, slightly malty, and delightfully sweet, with some fruit notes of papaya and mango, without the darker roasted notes of regular Assams.

When I first joined my father in his tea business in 1988, we offered the standard fare in black teas: a basic Darjeeling, an Earl Grey, an English Breakfast, and not much more. I suspected there had to be others out there. I got the chance to go looking in 1990, when we received a commission from the Japanese retailer Takashimaya to source rare teas for their new tea shop in New York. With their backing, I scoured the tea world and discovered this remarkable Assam.

Natural sweetness in tea comes from tips, or buds. The best Assam black teas have some golden tips, both to give them more elegance and to drive up their price. Indian tea makers are understandably reluctant to concentrate all their golden tips in a single tea, as they make more money by spreading them out. But Golden Tip Assam is pure golden tips. Created within just the last thirty years, the tea is so rare that it is made only on commission. I have to place an order before the harvest has even begun.

Golden Tip Assam comes from the Dikom tea estate, a garden in northern Assam known for its great Orthodox teas. Like all Assams, this tea has fairly blunt aromas from a very short withering. Unlike most Assams, however, Golden Tip is only barely rolled to preserve the delicate, expensive buds. The buds then oxidize to a beautiful gold color when they are transferred to an oven to dry.

With so many buds, this tea may scorch if brewed with fully boiling water. You may want to experiment with slightly lower temperatures to see what tastes best.

MANGALAM FTGFOP OR 815

*Mangalam Fancy Tippy Golden Flowery Orange
Pekoe Orthodox 815*

BREWING TEMPERATURE	212°F.
BREWING TIME	4–5 minutes.
DRY LEAVES	A mix of twisted burnt sienna leaves and golden buds, each about ½ inch long.
LIQUOR	Rich, red brown caramel.
AROMAS	Sweet and toasty, like toast spread with dark honey.
BODY	Full-bodied, though lighter than most Assams.
FLAVORS	Signature brisk, mellow toasted flavor like a dark honey or a light molasses.

This beautiful, potent tea is one of the best Orthodox Assams. Mangalam tea estate is named after Kumar Mangalam Birla, once the son of the estate's owners and now one of its managers. The estate is owned by Jayshree Tea & Industries, a large company that incorporated in 1945 and has tea gardens in Assam and Darjeeling. Jayshree is heralded in the Orthodox world for its special clones that produce a big golden leaf tip, which no one is able to replicate. You can identify Jayshree Assams by the tips' exquisite golden color.

The numbering system for this tea uses the letters OR, meaning Orthodox, followed by the lot number 815. Such a high number indicates that it was harvested during the Second Flush period.

The Second Flush period is arguably the best time for Assams. Assam producers tried to imitate Darjeeling First Flushes, but they were not successful with a lighter version of the region's tea. People just love the taste of this strong, sophisticated tea.

MANGALAM FTGBOP SPECIAL OR 555

Mangalam Fancy Tippy Golden Broken Orange
Pekoe Special Orthodox 555

BREWING TEMPERATURE	212°F.
BREWING TIME	4–5 minutes.
DRY LEAVES	The same leaves as Mangalam FTGFOP (page 146), only broken up (about ⅛ inch long) and duller in color.
LIQUOR	Darker red auburn brown.
AROMAS	Very dark, almost bittersweet caramel.
BODY	Full-bodied, more astringent than the previous tea.
FLAVORS	The malty flavor of roasted grains. Bittersweet.

This tea comes from the same garden and harvest as the preceding tea. Tasting the two next to each other helps illustrate how much leaf size helps determine a tea's characteristics: Briefly put, the smaller the leaf, the simpler and more assertive the flavors and aromas, and the darker the liquor. This tea is a Broken Orange Pekoe, while the previous one is graded Flowery. This one has the smaller leaves.

When the tea leaves are rolled, the rolling machine crushes at different rates, creating some longer leaves and some shorter. The previous tea is an example of the "fines," the first leaves to drop out of the machine. By contrast, this tea was put through a *dhool* and rolled again.

Both are excellent Assams, both have the lovely Mangalam flavors of malt and dark honey. This GBOP Special resembles its GFOP cousin, but this one emphasizes strength while the other shows off its sophistication. I drink a tea like this most mornings. I love its mixture of strength and dark honey flavors.

BOISAHABI CTC PF 642
Boisahabi CTC Pekoe Fannings Lot No. 642

BREWING TEMPERATURE	212°F.
BREWING TIME	4–5 minutes.
DRY LEAVES	Tiny, machine-made pellets, their color a dark brown, almost black.
LIQUOR	Dark red brown.
AROMAS	Assertive, sweet-charred aromas like roasted onions.
BODY	Robustly full-bodied—intensely astringent.
FLAVORS	Very steady, surprisingly consistent flavor.

While 95 percent of the teas on the market in India and Great Britain are CTC teas, this is the only one I'm including in the book. Obviously CTC teas are enjoyed by millions of people, but I feel the world of tea offers so much more. The aromas of CTC teas are simple and strong, with only a ghost of fruit flavors. The liquor is much darker, with much more body.

Though quite robust, this Boisahabi CTC is also palatable. When you taste this CTC, notice how uniform its flavors are in the mouth. Unlike Orthodox teas, CTC teas do not evolve and alter as you taste but remain consistent. The flavor is comfortingly stable but also somewhat predictable.

Boisahibi CTC comes from a particularly handsome garden in Assam that still has traces of British influence in its architecture. The flat fields are filled with thousands of tea plants, with tall shade trees rising high above them.

CEYLON BLACK TEAS

1. *New Vithanakande FBOP EX SP*

2. *Kenilworth BOP1*

3. *Uva Highlands Pekoe*

To the south and east of the Indian subcontinent lies the small, pear-shaped country of Sri Lanka. The tropical island is smaller than the state of Indiana yet produces a quantity and variety of black teas to rival China. Its unique topography and climate allow for three types of tea, determined not by season but by altitude: low-grown, medium-grown, and high-grown, each with its own unusual flavor profile.

Today, these teas are called Ceylons for marketing purposes; the island has not held the name of Ceylon since it was a British colony. Though the nation won independence in 1948, for the sake of recognizability, Sri Lankan tea makers have kept the name Ceylon for their teas.

The British brought the first tea plants to Sri Lanka at the end of the 1830s, shortly after establishing plantations in Assam and only a little while after seizing control of the island in 1815. Tea did not become one of the island's dominant crops until the 1870s, when blight wiped out the country's coffee plantations. Tea plants proved resistant to the coffee rust, so in the right order of things, tea replaced coffee. Entrepreneurial Scotsmen established the great plantations. Finding the mountains outside the commercial capital of Colombo similar to the Scottish Highlands, they gave their high, cool gardens the names of their homes: Kenilworth, Dunedin, Glasgow, and St. Andrews and St. Michaels. By the early 1900s, they had transformed Ceylon into a major tea source on a par with northeastern India. The Scot Sir Thomas Lipton made a fortune in Ceylon teas, taking advantage of industrialized production methods to mass-market one of the first cheap blends.

Today, Lipton, the tea company, plays only a small role in Sri Lanka; it sources mostly Kenya and Tanzania, as well as thirty-three other countries. However, Sri Lanka remains a major force in the industry. Belying its size, the island generates a massive quantity of tea. While most tea regions have one peak spring season, Ceylon has two, which allows it to grow tea almost year-round. The island is split down the middle by its Central Highlands, a mountain range with peaks upward of six thousand feet. From January to May, the teas on the western side of the island peak as monsoons batter the eastern side. While the churning clouds drench part of the island, they dry out the western half, drawing up moisture to generate the ideal dry, sunny weather for peak teas. From July to October, the situation reverses, and the eastern side peaks as monsoons soak the western half of the island. Whether peaking or not, in the tropical warmth tea grows all year, and so quickly that some gardens have to harvest the fresh leaves as often as every week. The gardens' yield per acre can be as much as thirty times that of the gardens in China or Japan. Depending on the year, Sri Lanka ranks as either the first or second largest tea exporter in the world, after—or before—China.

To cope with the bounty, Sri Lanka's tea gardens and factories are almost as organized and well run as the best in Japan. Ceylon tea marketing is also orderly and professional, with tea auctions most weeks in Colombo. The average Ceylon tea sells for much less than other British Legacy Teas, because the high volume has hurt the region's prestige. As a result, Ceylon tea makers who want to make money have been forced to innovate. The best tea makers now boast that every garden has its own recipe. From the cultivars to the withering, rolling, oxidation, and firing, every garden performs each step a little differently, resulting in an exquisite diversity of black teas.

The teas fall into three categories according to the elevation of their gardens. Low-grown teas come from the island's periphery, at elevations under two thousand feet. Submerged under tropical heat and humidity, most of these teas are dull and unremarkable, but New Vithanakande represents a chocolaty, honey-limned exception. Medium-grown teas flourish between two thousand and four thousand feet, where the cooler, drier climate produces fruitier, mellow teas like Kenilworth. The high-grown teas, between four thousand and six thousand feet, are what make Ceylon teas' reputation. That rarefied air produces exceptional teas like the wintergreen Uva Highlands. We will now taste all three, in order from mellowest to brightest and most vigorous.

NEW VITHANAKANDE FBOP EX SP
New Vithanakande Flowery Broken Orange Pekoe Extra Special

BREWING TEMPERATURE	212°F.
BREWING TIME	5 minutes.
DRY LEAVES	Narrow, twisted, very dark brown leaf segments about ⅓ inch long, with fine silver tips threaded in.
LIQUOR	Red brown.
AROMAS	A lovely blend of honey, unsweetened chocolate, and faint apricot notes.
BODY	Mouth-filling, full-bodied.
FLAVORS	An intense blend of unsweetened chocolate and honey sweetness, with a little lemony astringency.

While Darjeeling and Assam teas suffer from hyperbole, the labels on Ceylon teas are more reliable. New Vithanakande FBOP EX SP is truly special—indeed, astonishing.

Sri Lanka's low-grown teas are generally quite poor; the region lies only three hundred feet above sea level, and in the tropical heat and humidity, the teas become dark and unremarkable. Most are sold for negligible amounts as bulk teas. To make any money, the low-altitude Ratnapura district tea gardens had to innovate. Some entrepreneurs figured out a way to keep the tips white, and now the district is famous for its silver tippy teas. New Vithanakande is the best of the bunch, with small leaves like most Broken Orange Pekoe teas, yet flowery with the most unlikely of black tea components: silver tips. Ordinarily, tea tips turn golden yellow during black tea production. New Vithanakande preserves the tips' silver hue.

The tea makers begin by withering the leaves very briefly, then rolling them for just fifteen minutes, using hardly any pressure on the leaves. Instead of rolling them on a table between pressurized disks, they pour the leaves into a vertical cylinder with a sieve at its base. As the cylinder slowly spins, the leaves rub up against and lightly macerate one another. Kept whole and undamaged, the tips don't oxidize while the rest of the leaves do. Thus the tips stay a shiny silver.

As the leaves jostle about, the finest, smallest, and most delicate ones fall through the sieve. The rest of the leaves—about 99.5 percent of them—are transferred to a rolling machine to become ordinary bulk low-grown tea. The smallest and most delicate leaves are left to oxidize for about two hours, much more than most Ceylon teas. They are also blasted with moist air of the sort that jets from a humidifier. This moist air may provoke the leaves to form their characteristic cocoa and chocolate flavors. I only speculate, as the same humidifying treatment is afforded Keemun Chinese black teas, which have similar cocoa notes (see "Keemun Mao Feng," page 112, and "Keemun Hao Ya A," page 114). Like Keemuns, the New Vithanakande teas are fired at a hotter temperature than other Ceylon teas, which likely creates a Maillard reaction to reinforce the cocoa flavors.

After firing, the tea makers spread out the leaves on a fine-mesh strainer and sort through them by hand. Every other British Legacy Tea is processed entirely by machine, but the makers of New Vithanakande sift the leaves, gently working the smallest particles through the strainer. The silver tips are larger and remain with the tea; the smaller golden tips fall through to the floor. The result is a delicious, surprisingly engaging low-grown tea, as beautiful to look at as to drink.

KENILWORTH BOP1
Kenilworth Broken Orange Pekoe No. 1

BREWING TEMPERATURE	212°F.
BREWING TIME	5 minutes.
DRY LEAVES	Brown black, elegantly twisted leaves with some red along the edges; between ¼ and 1 inch long. No tips.
LIQUOR	Rose brown.
BODY	Mellow, medium-bodied.
AROMAS	Sharp, bright notes of wood and warm honey.
BODY	Medium, much lighter than other teas from Sri Lanka or Assam.
FLAVORS	Much mellower than the aromas; though somewhat astringent, the tea has rounded, gentle roasted flavors, with hints of peach and clover honey in the finish.

This medium-bodied middle-grown tea has a wonderfully easygoing nature. The Kenilworth tea estate is one of the oldest in Sri Lanka, established by a Scot in the nineteenth century. Halfway up Sri Lanka's Central Highlands, at an elevation of roughly two thousand feet, the temperatures are not as hot as low-grown tea areas, but the Kenilworth estate is still hotter and more humid than the high-grown areas in the Highlands' peaks. Typical medium-grown teas like Kenilworth are soothingly mellow, yet still assertively brisk.

Kenilworth teas peak in the spring, when the monsoons douse the other half of the island with rain. The monsoons draw moisture out of the air around the garden, concentrating the flavors in the tea leaves. After harvesting, tea makers at Kenilworth give their leaves a medium wither, in contrast with the light withering of Assams and the hard withering of Darjeelings. To macerate the leaves, they use Orthodox rolling machines, but at a faster pace and for a longer period than any other Ceylon teas—two hours. In another unusual step, the rolled leaves are distributed onto trays that circulate for another two hours on a moving belt that snakes around the room. After oxidizing 100 percent, the leaves are dried in ovens at a hotter temperature than that for high-grown teas. The thorough rolling, oxidation, and intense firing help reinforce the mellow, baked flavors that make this one of the most famous teas in Sri Lanka.

UVA HIGHLANDS PEKOE

BREWING TEMPERATURE	212°F.
BREWING TIME	3–4 minutes.
DRY LEAVES	A rotovaned tea; the dried leaf particles are very small and choppy, though not quite as small or uniform as a CTC tea, and with a lovely reddish dark brown cast.
LIQUOR	Red brown.
AROMAS	Wintergreen.
BODY	Quite brisk, filling your mouth with tingles.
FLAVORS	Wintergreen, with lovely black Ceylon tea flavors in the background.

Sri Lanka produces an incredible array of teas within a surprisingly confined area in the highest parts of country's Central Highlands. A two-hour drive will take you from Dimbulla, an estate famous for malty, thick, dark-colored brews, to Nuwara Eliya, a gorgeous spot whose cluster of tea gardens is renowned for light-colored liquors and lemony, floral aromas. The teas from both gardens are all worth trying. I had difficulty choosing which high-altitude tea to include in the book; because of its unique wintergreen flavor, I have picked this one from the garden called Uva Highlands.

Uva Highlands Pekoe comes from the mountain peaks of the Uva district, about 3,600 feet above sea level. Set on the western side of Sri Lanka's Central Highlands, Uva Highlands estate makes its teas during the dry season in August and September, when the mountains block the monsoon rains buffeting the eastern side of the island. Because of both the varietal and the way it is processed, during the tea making the leaves produce an "ester," or aromatic compound, called "methyl salicylate" that offers a minty fresh taste.

To concentrate the tea's flavors, Uva Highlands takes advantage of the cold mountain air and processes its teas in the middle of the night, starting at about one in the morning. The estate does a hard wither for about eighteen hours, making the leaves crackly dry. Then it rolls the leaves in an Orthodox rolling machine, macerating them thoroughly. Finally, it decimates the leaves in a roto-vane, a machine resembling an airplane propeller, which shreds the leaves not once but twice, reducing them to a doughy green pulp. The decimation makes the tea heartily brisk, or "gutty," as it's called in the tea world.

The mass of pulverized leaves is spread out on raised tiles, where it oxidizes for about an hour and a half. The relatively brief oxidation gives the leaves a charmingly lighter hue. It also draws out the lovely wintergreen flavor and aroma. To preserve these scents and tastes, the company fires the leaves in the oven at a lower temperature than that of other regions. The light firing protects the volatile compounds, rather than masking them with additional heat flavors.

KENYAN BLACK TEAS

1. *Milima GFBOP1*

I wish I could offer more Kenyan black teas, but only a tiny fraction of the country's pure, Orthodox teas are good enough to drink on their own. As opposed to the centralized tea estates of India and Sri Lanka, and the small gardens of China and Japan, in Kenya tea production is scattered among nearly half a million small farmers, all operating independently. This huge number makes quality control an almost insurmountable challenge. The lion's share of the tea is turned into CTC pellets, added to blends, and packaged in teabags. Hardly any of these blends are even marketed as Kenyan tea.

Kenyans have cultivated tea since the early 1900s, when the British established the first tea plantations in what was then their colony. By the 1920s, the British were manufacturing African tea commercially, and by the 1950s, after South Asia had won its independence from Great Britain, Kenya supplied the British with the bulk of their tea. Today, the equatorial African country still provides Great Britain with over 40 percent of its black teas and is the fourth largest producer of tea after China, Sri Lanka, and India. The largest tea-growing areas lie in the southwestern part of the country, west of the Rift Valley in the Kenyan Highlands. There, tea thrives in the cool air at elevations more than six thousand feet above sea level, peaking during the February dry season.

To command higher prices, a small cohort of Kenyan tea makers has begun experimenting with Orthodox pure teas, both white and black. I look forward to enjoying the results. Though quality is on the rise, the finest pure teas from Kenya are not yet on a par with the best from South Asia. The best I've found so far is the following Milima Broken Orange Pekoe from the Kenyan Highlands, with charming orange and spice notes to make it a tea to watch.

MILIMA GFBOP1

Milima Golden Flowery Broken Orange Pekoe No. 1

BREWING TEMPERATURE	212°F.
BREWING TIME	5 minutes.
DRY LEAVES	Small leaf particles of a dark, rich brown, sprinkled with pieces of gold tip.
LIQUOR	Deep reddish brown.
AROMAS	A mixture of lemon and grass, with faint clove notes.
BODY	Medium full.
FLAVORS	Tending toward citrus, especially orange, with a slightly spicy character of cloves and some pepper.

Milima is Swahili for "In a High Place." The tea plants that produce this tea grow more than six thousand feet above sea level in the Kenyan Highlands. The leaves take on lovely flavors in the cool air and rocky soil. Milima is a pure black tea made from a blend of leaves from three gardens belonging to the British James Finlay Tea Company. The leaves are brought to the Marinyn estate, where the teas are withered, rolled in the Orthodox fashion between two plates, oxidized, and dried, all in the manner of British Legacy Teas. The quality varies from year to year; at its peak, Milima offers charming citrus and spice aromas and flavors.

BRITISH BLACK TEA BLENDS

1. *English Breakfast*

2. *Earl Grey*

Tea makers have been blending teas for centuries, mixing them with other teas or with flavored additives like rose petals, cinnamon, and jasmine blossoms to amplify their flavors. The British expanded this practice in the nineteenth century, when the Lipton, Twinings, and other tea companies created blends of Chinese and Indian teas for everyday drinkers. We'll try two of them now.

In spite of their popularity, most flavored teas are to pure teas what wine coolers are to fine wines. The added flavors mask the nuance in the leaves. When you drink a pure tea, wonderful things happen in your mouth as the flavors alter and evolve. With additives, the flavor is more often constant and unchanging.

That constancy holds tremendous appeal, for both the tea drinker and the manufacturer. Flavored teas are cheaper and easier to produce: Since the added flavors make up most of the taste, they require lesser grades of tea. It's much easier to control the quality of the additives than it is to control the tea. You can control pure tea as well as you can control Mother Nature. As with the best wines and their vintages, some years are better than others.

Pure tea is an adventure; to help inspire you to keep exploring, we will now investigate two blends that I hope you'll treat as a launch pad into the less familiar pure teas that go into them.

ENGLISH BREAKFAST

BREWING TEMPERATURE	212°F.
BREWING TIME	5 minutes.
DRY LEAVES	While many versions of this blend are made with CTC pellets, try to get one made from Orthodox, fuller black leaves.
LIQUOR	Dark brown.
AROMAS	The Harney & Sons blend has a toasty aroma from its mix of Chinese black teas; other blends have the sharper, spicier nose of British Legacy Teas.
BODY	Full.
FLAVORS	Varies with the version; in general a good English Breakfast should be straightforward, with hints of orange, clove, smoke, and a little honey.

English Breakfast was designed as a simple tea for the average middle-class citizen to start the day, and for about the first hundred years of its existence, the tea was brewed by British tea makers from Chinese black teas. Toward the end of the nineteenth century, as the new British tea barons started to make their own tea in India, a huge marketing effort was launched to get the English to switch to the new South Asian tea flavors. It took a while, but in time the English accepted the brisker, stronger flavors of the Indian teas, and now they reject the milder versions made with Chinese blacks.

My father learned the tea business from an old English tea man named Stanley Mason. Mason got his start in the tea trade when Britannia still ruled the waves and made an English Breakfast with Chinese black tea. We've continued to have success with Mason's mixture ever since my father started his own tea operation in 1970. It was only when my father and I started exporting Mason's blend to hotels back in England that we hit a snag. In Great Britain, our tea was considered too weak. It also had a slightly smoky flavor that our British clients found unpleasant. I explored the inner workings of strong English teas. What made that spoon stand up? After several trials, I created a more "English" English Breakfast with more robust British Legacy Teas. Since then, I have never heard a complaint, and in fact this blended tea helped the Dorchester Hotel win the United Kingdom Tea Council's award for "London's Top Tea."

Whatever the version, an English Breakfast blend can serve as a wonderful launching point for a voyage through tea. If you like a traditional English Breakfast made of Chinese black teas, try some of the other China blacks: Keemun Hao Ya A or the lighter version, Keemun Mao Feng. From there, sample some Yunnan black teas. If you like Yunnans, you might also try puerhs, the aged teas made from them. Another path might lead toward the darker oolongs such as Da Hong Pao or Bai Hao. Those two might lead to the lighter oolongs: Ti Guan Yin and Ali Shan. From there, jump into China's fabulous green teas.

If you prefer a brisker, more "English" English Breakfast, taste some Assams and Ceylons before sampling Darjeelings. You may prefer darker, Second Flush Darjeelings; if so, try Bai Hao, which has a similar dark stone fruit flavor. If you like the greener First Flush Darjeelings, it is a short trip over to Japanese Senchas— the Japanese are big buyers of First Flush Darjeelings, so they have pushed the Indians to make it similar to Sencha. As you can see, English Breakfast is a great base camp for your explorations.

EARL GREY

BREWING TEMPERATURE	212°F.
BREWING TIME	4–5 minutes.
DRY LEAVES	The dark brown leaves will vary widely depending on the version, from tiny pellets to long twists. The larger the leaves the better.
LIQUOR	Reddish brown to dark brown black, depending on the blend.
AROMAS	Bergamot, a lovely sweet citrus aroma with honey notes.
BODY	Full.
FLAVORS	Identical to the aroma, with a pleasantly robust, astringent bite in the finish.

Though this book is a guide to pure tea, I wanted to include the Earl Grey blend since it is one of the most widely known teas in the Western world. I like to think of it as a gateway tea for novice palates. Though its profile comes as much from added bergamot oil as from tea leaves, the best versions incorporate delicious black teas from all over the world; once you feel comfortable with this blend, you can explore the pure black teas on their own.

Every tea company has its own version and guards its recipes, but traditionally Earl Grey is made from both Indian and Chinese teas, which are blended in a drum with bergamot oil extracted from the citrus peel. (Bergamot is a citrus native to Italy, a pear-shaped orange that tastes very much the way Earl Grey smells.)

The famous English tea company Twinings is credited with inventing the blend. The tea is named after the second Earl Grey. His father, the first Earl Grey (Charles Grey), was a famous (or infamous) general on the British side during the American Revolution. In gratitude for his service, King George III elevated the general into the peerage with the title of Earl. "Grey" is thus a family surname, not a place; that is why the tea's name is Earl Grey, not Earl of Grey. The second Earl Grey ruled as prime minister of the United Kingdom from 1830 to 1834. The story of the tea goes that while Grey served as prime minister, a Chinese mandarin sent him some scented tea as a gift. When the prime minister ran out of the tea, he asked the Twinings tea company to replicate it. The tale seems a little tall: Bergamot is native to Italy, not China, and although the Chinese flavor their teas with plenty of other fruits and blossoms (see "Dragon Pearl Jasmine," page 47), I have never seen a Chinese black tea flavored with bergamot.

Legends aside, Earl Grey remains a popular blend. In my family's version, which we call Earl Grey Supreme, we use some of our favorite black, oolong, and even white teas. Ours has the toasty smoothness of Keemun, the heft of a strong Assam, the briskness and aroma of high-grown Ceylons, the roasted stone fruit flavor and lightness of Formosa Oolong, and the sweetness and beauty of a white Yin Zhen. Each component offers an avenue to discover those teas on their own, each sip of Earl Grey enticing you to explore the enchantments of pure tea.

PUERHS

1. *Ban-Zhang 2004 Green Ping Cha*

2. *Loose-Leafed Black Puerh*

3. *Tuo Cha 1991 Yunnan Tea Import & Export Corporation*

ith every other category of tea in this book, tea brokers perform something of a race to get the tea from factory to pot. The aromas and flavors of fresh teas are so volatile, even when vacuum-packed in airtight foil, most teas start to lose their sparkle within a matter of months. Many green teas and oolongs are gone before a year, black teas within a year or two. Puerhs are different. Puerh makers finish making the tea, set the leaves in cakes on shelves, and wait anywhere from two to fifty years before drinking a cup.

Pronounced "POOH-airs," these are aged teas. Their prolonged resting periods give the teas their own class of extraordinarily earthy flavors. No other teas taste of tobacco, or musk, or even dirt.

I've put them last in the book in part because they are so robust; as with any tea tasting, we begin with the lightest tea and end with the strongest. Puerhs also close the book because they are the farthest removed from the pure tea leaf.

Puerhs get their unusual qualities from fermentation, a process no other tea endures. (While it is common to credit fermentation for turning green teas black, that browning process is in fact called "oxidation.") The science of the puerh fermentation is not much understood outside of China, but we can speculate that fungal and bacterial microbes in the air likely go to work on the leaves in much the way that yeasts act on wine grapes or sourdough starters alter bread dough. These microbes convert starches and other compounds in the leaves from simple sugars into the wonderfully named "monoterpenoids," which in turn oxidize and degrade over the years into "sesquiterpenoids." Sesquiterpenoid compounds are known for their earthy and camphor flavors.

For many tea drinkers, these musky flavors make puerhs an acquired taste. It's no surprise the teas are among the most popular in two cities known for their unusual foods—Guangzhou (formerly Canton) and Hong Kong. Those who do acquire the taste often become unusually, almost spiritually, devoted to the tea.

The tea gets its name from Puerh county in China's Yunnan province, where the style likely originated. In the Tang dynasty (618–907), the region became the starting point for the Tea-Horse Roads, trade routes for tea, horses, and other commodities between China and the Mongols in Tibet. One of the better stories claims that the teas fermented by accident while strapped to the horses during the long journey across the Tibetan plateau. Puerhs remain popular in Tibet today.

Puerhs are prized throughout China as slimming teas. While there are no conclusive studies to prove this, the tea is often said to reduce cholesterol and blood pressure. China's Yunnan Tea Branch, a prestigious producer of puerhs, also boasts that the tea "quickens your recovery from intoxication." The company has plenty of experience with the tea, having made puerhs since the company was first established in 1944.

In large part because of its health benefits, the tea has become extraordinarily popular throughout Asia in just the last five years. The tea has seen a big surge in value, to the point where investors now speculate in puerhs. Unfortunately, the speculation has also attracted counterfeiters. It is possible to find a puerh as much as fifty years old, but the older they get, the more likely they are to be fake. It is crucial to buy from reputable sources that get their puerhs from the better factories in Yunnan such as the Yunnan Tea Branch.

The very best puerhs are made from large-leafed tea plants native to Yunnan (see "Yunnan Black Tea," page 115). The leaves are processed in one of two ways: green or raw (*sheng*) and a more recent style, black or cooked (*shou*).

Green puerhs are the most traditional form of the tea. The leaves are fixed green on a hot surface after harvesting, withered until they grow limp, then steamed hot and compressed into cakes. The cakes are wrapped in paper and left to age for anywhere from two to fifty years. It's possible to buy young green puerhs and age them at home: Keep the cakes in a cool, dry place, away from mildew and damp and out of the sun, and they should last for just over a decade.

Black puerhs are an innovation of just the last few decades. To meet an increasing demand for the tea, researchers found a way to make a sort of imitation puerh that does not require aging. I explain more about this science in the entry on the tea "Loose-Leafed Black Puerh," page 179.

Both types come in a charming variety of shapes. In green puerhs, the shapes influence the rate and quality of the aging; in black teas, the shapes are just for decoration. They range from *bing cha*, a flat round disk, to *fang cha*, a square brick; *tuan cha*, a melon; and even *jin cha*, a mushroom. There's also *ping cha*, which means "iron tea"—a cake so compact that it's as solid as iron and is actually hard to break off. But *ping cha* also boasts even more nuanced characteristics from aging and oxidizing that much more slowly.

As a result of their cake form, with the exception of a few loose-leafed black puerhs, you cannot scoop this tea into a pot with a teaspoon. To brew the tea, begin by breaking off a small chunk of the cake. The cakes can be fairly stiff; if you cannot break off a piece with your hands, use a blunt knife or letter opener to jimmy off a square. You can buy a special puerh knife for this purpose, but a regular table knife works fine. Since the ratio of tea to water is the same with puerhs as with every other tea, break off about 1 rounded teaspoon's worth of the cake for 1 cup.

Unlike every other tea leaves, puerh leaves require rinsing to open up their flavors. Set the piece in your brewing vessel, pour in boiling water, and let stand for 30 to 45 seconds before draining. Wait a few seconds to let the drained tea awaken.

You can make just a single cup or you can brew the leaves up to a dozen times. As with oolongs, with each round it is fascinating to observe how certain flavors emerge as others disappear. Traditionally, each brew is poured out into puerh tasting cups. Though each contains only a few thimblefuls' worth of liquor, after twelve of them you will feel quite alert. Puerh devotees call the buzzing sensation "puerh intoxication."

There are many different ways to brew puerhs. Whether for a mug or a round of small cups, brew the first batch in boiling water for 1 to 3 minutes. For subsequent brews, start by steeping the tea for just 10 seconds, increasing the time by a few seconds for up to a dozen rounds. (Puerh fans sometimes time it by a number of breaths, but breaths can be so variable, seconds are more reliable.)

What follows are three puerhs of varying styles. We'll start with a young, bright three-year-old green puerh that still has some sweetness and fruit. Next comes a blunt, earthy black puerh typical of the more recent mock-aged style. The chapter ends with a robust, rounded fifteen-year-old green puerh, a nice example of an aged puerh, full of ripe earthy flavors. Don't worry if you cannot find these exact varieties; just look for a young green puerh, a black puerh, and a true aged green puerh, and the descriptors should still help you understand the general categories.

BAN-ZHANG 2004 GREEN PING CHA

BREWING TEMPERATURE	212°F.
BREWING TIME	1–3 minutes for the first round; 10+ seconds thereafter.
DRY LEAVES	A compressed 8-inch disk about 1 inch thick, with swirls of lighter golden buds threaded through the dark green leaves.
LIQUOR	Yellow brown; darker with subsequent brews.
AROMAS	A heady mixture of fruit, woods, and spice.
BODY	Moderately full-bodied.
FLAVORS	Fruit notes of raspberry jam, along with tobacco and earthy flavors of must and dry leaves. The enduring finish has a nice spicy quality, evocative of camphor.

A characteristic young green puerh, Ban-Zhang Green Ping Cha can also be aged at home. Like a young Bordeaux wine, it is drinkable now, but its best days are ahead of it. While it has nice fruit flavors in its young state, age will help mellow and round those out, giving the tea greater nuance and polish.

Like a great French wine, this tea comes from one of the finest puerh "châteaus." But unlike a Lafite or Latour, this name is a little more cumbersome: the Yunnan Tea Branch of the China National Native Produce & Animal By-Products Import & Export Corporation. As the awkward title suggests, the company is a relic of Communist China's old ways before it began privatizing many tea companies just a few years ago. But unlike most state-run tea operations, the Yunnan Tea Branch is a reliable company, producing some of the best puerhs in the world.

This tea is made in Ban-Zhang, a mountainous region in southwestern Yunnan province, close to Burma. Yunnan is thought to be the region where tea plants first emerged; near Ban-Zhang, centuries-old wild tea trees still grow, many of them up to thirty feet high. The tea bushes for the puerh teas are tended by a local ethnic minority called the Hanai, and the puerhs are made in a particular style. After the leaves are fixed and partially dried, they are shipped to the Yunnan Tea Branch, where they are fully dried and formed into cakes. The Yunnan Tea Branch holds on to the cakes a little longer before selling them, to allow the rawness to dissipate and the fermentation to begin.

More and more puerh drinkers in China and elsewhere are collecting and then aging these teas at home. The best way to age Ping Cha is to keep it in a dry room away from strong smells and let it sit there for ten to fifteen years. Of course, it can also be drunk sooner, if you run out of patience.

LOOSE-LEAFED BLACK PUERH

BREWING TEMPERATURE   212°F.

BREWING TIME   1–3 minutes for the first round; 10+ seconds thereafter.

DRY LEAVES   A loose-leafed puerh with small, thoroughly twisted brown leaves and a few golden tips. The tips give the leaves a light film of dust.

LIQUOR   Inky: dark and murky. With multiple brews, the color lightens.

AROMAS   Dirt and ash.

BODY   Light.

FLAVORS   Earthy, robust, and blunt. The earthy flavors recede slightly and the tea mellows with more brews. Dark plummy flavors slowly emerge, with some sweetness poking out by the third brew.

Often marketed simply as "puerh," this black, or *shou,* puerh illustrates a style invented in the early 1970s to imitate the affects of aging. True aged puerhs are so rare that black puerh is now the most common style found in the United States.

With the demand for puerhs on the rise, tea makers at the famous Menghai Tea Factory discovered a way to speed up the aging process. Instead of aging fixed green teas, tea makers oxidize them to anywhere from 40 to 90 percent. Then they put the tea through *wo dui,* or "moist track." They pile the oxidized leaves into heaps, where bacteria and fungi decay them at an accelerated rate, just as in my compost pile. After a few months, leaves are fired to stop the oxidation and the decay and to compress the leaves into cakes.

Black puerhs have plenty of charm, but they lack the nuance and depth of true aged green puerhs. While this tea has strong earthy, ashy flavors, it has a thinner body and a sharper edge than the aged Tuo Cha, following.

TUO CHA 1991 YUNNAN TEA IMPORT & EXPORT CORPORATION

Bowl Tea

BREWING TEMPERATURE	212°F.
BREWING TIME	2 minutes.
DRY LEAVES	A tea cake about 3 inches in diameter, shaped like half of a hollow globe or thick-sided bowl. The surface is slightly smoothed, with the occasional stem and irregular leaf poking out.
LIQUOR	Dark red brown.
AROMAS	Dry leaves; mildly earthy; with more brews, scents of fruits and spice emerge.
BODY	Medium.
FLAVORS	A tobacco sweetness, like pipe ash.

Although Tuo Cha has recently become all the rage in France and Spain as European women drink it to keep from getting fat, Tuo Cha also provides all the rich flavors of a true aged green puerh. At the time I tasted it for this chapter, it was fifteen years old.

Fifteen years in a cool, dry room have given these tea leaves pleasurable earthy flavors, with no trace of the fruit sweetness of the young Ban-Zhang Green Ping Cha (page 177). The time has also turned the once fixed green leaves a solid, mesmerizingly deep and shiny black color. The tea has a seductive mellowness, a smooth, rounded quality from its years sitting quietly fermenting. Its leaves are almost impenetrably dark, its liquor equally so.

This tea can be rebrewed as many as a dozen times. The later brews are mellow but thin in body, lighter in color but with sweeter notes, especially in the finish.

THE FUTURE OF TEA

rom puerhs to white teas, from tobacco to honeysuckle: I hope by now you have relished the spectacular range of flavors of pure tea, and feel confident to call yourself a connoisseur. My goal has been to guide you through the incredible variety that's become available to tea drinkers since I entered the business, to help you enjoy tea that much more. Few of these teas were available in the West when my family started working in the industry forty years ago. Since then, high-mountain oolongs have emerged from Taiwan and white teas from Sri Lanka. Darjeelings brightened, Assams lightened; how could the tea world possibly get any better? All that remains is to continue supporting these innovative tea makers by drinking their creations.

The best tea is a miracle of Mother Nature and of human ingenuity. We can treat tea as we would cherish a good summer tomato or a ripe peach. We can drink it when it's in season: spring teas when they come ready in the summer, summer teas in the fall, and autumnal teas in the winter to tide us over to spring again. In Japan, tea stores stretch banners across their storefronts in the early summer proclaiming the arrival of the Sencha harvest. I have a banner to display in my store—but it's in Japanese. I'd love to see more versions in English.

We can study tea the way we research fine wines and get to know its *terroir*. We can make it a priority to know exactly where it's made and the people who make it. We can speak of Yoshihiro Matsuda with the same reverence we reserve for the makers of great wines. We can encourage the incipient movement toward sustainable tea cultivation, supporting tea makers who nurture their plants using organic methods. Tea currently lags behind other agricultural products in this area, but more gardens convert to organic each year.

Cultivating a palate for better tea can also help protect the beverage. These teas often come from poorer areas of the world threatened by development. The hills south of Taipei in Taiwan were once carpeted in tea fields; today, they're stacked with office buildings. In the British Legacy areas, tea makers can often make more money in industries like banking and software. The same pressures exist in China: It can be more rewarding to trade widgets in Shanghai than to run a tea plantation in Anxi, a poor and rural part of the country.

China in particular is at a real crossroads. In the last ten years, the Communist regime has moved to privatize much of its tea industry, allowing families and farmers to operate small-scale businesses of their own. The improvement in quality has been dramatic. To appeal to an ever richer domestic market, these private tea makers have been inventing new teas every year. Many have tinkered with making green versions of black teas, like green Keemuns, and black versions of greens, like an oxidized Lung Ching. Let's help them along.

It's been wonderful to watch the thirst for tea increase so much in the United States. Granted, much of the interest stems from tea's many health benefits, both as an antioxidant and as a more soothing stimulant than coffee. I'm happy for any reason people may have to drink more tea—but, unfortunately, the true extent of its health benefits has yet to be established. We cannot state categorically that tea prevents cancer or cardiovascular disease. It is safe to say that its polyphenols act as antioxidants, but scientists are still determining what antioxidants do. The catechins appear to reduce the effects of *free radicals*, molecules that may impede the healthy expression of DNA. Thus tea may help stave off cancer and heart disease. Indeed, recent studies suggest that the antioxidants in green tea are so effective, it may not be a good idea to take herbal supplements containing green tea extracts. These extracts may actually trigger too much of a response, in essence providing too much of a good thing.

Health seekers can also overlook black tea as a source of antioxidants. Though green teas contain more polyphenols than black teas, blacks contain their fair share. Only a portion degrade to theaflavins and thearubigins during the oxidation that turns green teas black—and these theaflavins and thearubigins seem to have some healthy properties of their own. Some claim that the antioxidant properties in tea may be inhibited if milk is added, but this also is not true. Black tea may not contain quite as many antioxidants as green tea, but it's still good for you.

In my ideal tea world, tea drinkers will know the joys of pure teas. A large portion of the tea consumed in the United States is blended or flavored. Many tea manufacturers boast of tea sommeliers or artful mixologists of tea and additives. The blending tradition stretches back centuries in China, where tea makers often mixed their leaves with blossoms, spices, and dried fruits. Flavored teas can be wonderful: They provide the tea maker opportunities for creativity in layering citrus, rose, coconut, or spice notes along with the tea. All those diverting flavors, however, often mask the true flavors of tea.

To help you continue tasting, I've created the "Tea-Tasting Menus" appendix, containing more advanced comparisons for you to try. I've grouped together the finest green and black spring teas, for example, as well as teas sweetened with buds and teas heavily smoked during their firings. This way, you can compare teas across varieties: a spring green tea against a spring black, for example, or a heavily fired tea with one that has no fired flavor at all. To broaden your understanding, I've also provided appendixes on the science and history of tea. Knowing the whys to tea's flavors will strengthen your palate. Understanding how British Legacy Teas came to be more heavily rolled than Chinese black teas will refine your ability to discern the teas' flavors. Just remember, this is not an exam: The ultimate goal of perceiving these flavors is to make you smile. And I hope, over the course of these last nine chapters, that I've given you plenty of reasons to grin.

APPENDIX

Tea-Tasting Menus

Although I've organized the book by styles of tea, many individual teas within each style resemble one another in unexpected ways. I've compiled a few lists to give you some ideas of other comparisons you might try.

TIPPY TEAS

These teas all have high numbers of sweet buds, or tips, the incipient leaves that some say are the most prized part of the plant. You can experience how tips lighten a black tea by comparing these three against each other. Yin Zhen is a white tea made entirely of tips; Golden Monkey is a Chinese black tea merely sweetened with tips, while Golden Tip Assam black tea contains tips alone.

- Yin Zhen white tea, page 21
- Golden Monkey Chinese black tea, page 107
- Golden Tip Assam black tea, page 144

SPRING TEAS

I dream of a day when we drink teas when they are in season. Spring teas are among the best of all teas, flush with nutrients to help the plants recover from their winter dormancy. They usually become available in midsummer. Here are four of the best spring teas in the world, from all over the world: two greens and two blacks.

- Bi Lo Chun Chinese green tea, page 37
- Matsuda's Sencha Japanese green tea, page 57
- Panyong Congou Chinese black tea, page 110
- Singbulli SFTGFOP1 Supreme Dj 18 Darjeeling black tea, page 130

MIDSUMMER TEAS

After the burst of life in the springtime, tea plants quiet down and produce more subdued brews. These two teas take advantage of naturally occurring herbivores to boost the flavors in the leaves. Though one is an oolong from Taiwan and the other a black tea from India, they have charming similarities.

- Bai Hao, aka Fanciest Formosa Oolong, page 91
- Margaret's Hope FTGFOP Muscatel Dj 275 Darjeeling black tea, page 133

BROTHY TEAS

These two teas are packed with amino acids; each has profoundly satisfying mouth-filling qualities.

- Taiping HouKui Chinese green tea, page 45
- Matsuda's Sencha Japanese green tea, page 57

CHOCOLATY TEAS

These teas contain more than average amounts of certain amino acids that help generate surprisingly chocolaty flavors. They don't taste like fudge, but they have the roasted flavors of barely sweetened cocoa powder. Though one is from China and the other India, their production methods are remarkably similar, designed to play up these cocoa notes.

- Keemun Hao Ya A Chinese black tea, page 114
- New Vithanakande Ceylon black tea, page 156

FLORAL TEAS

To discover the range of flavors possible in pure tea, it's fun to compare a tea flavored with flowers with one in which floral aromas occur naturally.

- Osmanthus oolong, page 88, versus Golden Monkey Chinese black tea, page 107
- Dragon Pearl Jasmine Chinese green tea, page 47, versus Ti Guan Yin oolong, page 86

HIGH-ALTITUDE TEAS

Some of the most intensely flavored teas come from some of the highest regions in the world. Here we have a Taiwanese oolong with gardenia flavors and a Ceylon black tea with aromas of wintergreen.

- Ali Shan oolong, page 81
- Uva Highlands Pekoe Ceylon black tea, page 160

THE INFLUENCE OF FIRING ON TEA

To understand how firing, the final stage of tea preparation, can affect flavor, compare Tencha, a Japanese green tea that is not fired at all, with Gunpowder, one of the most heavily fired Chinese green teas.

- Tencha Japanese green tea, page 70
- Gunpowder Chinese green tea, page 49

❧ SMOKY TEAS ❧

Once upon a time, teas were so heavily fired that they tasted of pine smoke. A few still do. These are two of the tea world's most intensely smoky varieties.

- Da Hong Pao oolong, page 93
- Lapsang Souchong Chinese black tea, page 117

APPENDIX

From Tree to Tea:

The Chemistry of Tea

hile the transformation of tea from bitter, waxy leaves on a bush to liquor in a pot may seem absurdly magical, tea makers actually follow the same basic steps worked out by farmers in China by the eighteenth century. To cultivate a taste for tea, it helps to understand the stages of tea production, as each phase contributes to the final taste. I have tried to write this out in the simplest possible language, since some of the scientific terminology may vex those (like me) for whom Chemistry 101 is a distant memory. Tea science is a burgeoning field; few resources have been dedicated to understanding the chemistry behind its flavor. Sometimes it can seem as though the conclusions change with every new study. From what little we do know, however, the science of tea can enthrall. Understanding these transformations will expand your palate. Consider this appendix, then, Tea Chemistry 101 and Palate Cultivation 202.

❧ HARVEST ❧

Flavor begins in the fields. Scientists have identified over six hundred flavors and aromas in tea, many with obscure and wonderful names like "linalool" and "hexanol." The miracle is that tea makers create these hundreds of flavors from only six classes of chemical compounds that all reside within the tea plant: color pigments, sugars, amino acids, fatty acids, caffeine, and polyphenols. These compounds exist in nature to nourish and protect the plant against attack. The aromas and flavors we find so enticing in tea actually deter aphids, leafhoppers, and other insects from eating the leaves. In essence, tea makers pose as insects, damaging the leaves to provoke them to defend themselves—and, in the process, rendering them delicious.

The first secret to flavorful tea is to gather the leaves at their peak, when they contain these compounds in the most mouthwatering proportions. With the exception of tropical teas from Assam and Ceylon, the finest teas peak in the spring.

Like all plants, tea bushes grow through photosynthesis. The color pigments chlorophyll and carotene absorb sunlight so that the plant can convert carbon dioxide and water into glucose and other sugars. When the sun fades in the winter, the bushes go dormant, storing nutrients in their roots. As the winter dormancy ends and the temperature warms, the plants draw on these nutrients to create more leaves. The plant forges amino acids to build proteins. And it produces caffeine and polyphenols to repel bugs and protect the plant from attack. The two chemicals appear to disorient herbivores, dissuading them from eating the leaves.

Caffeine and polyphenols are likely of most interest to the tea drinker from a practical standpoint. After all, many of us drink the beverage every morning for its ability to wake us up. And a growing percentage drink it to stay healthy, although the "health via antioxidants" claim remains inconclusive. It is safe to say that the polyphenols in tea act as antioxidants, but scientists are still establishing what antioxidants do. They appear to reduce the effects of free radicals, molecules that may interfere with the healthy expression of DNA, provoking the mutations that may lead to tumors. Thus tea may help stave off cancer as well as heart disease. We just don't know for sure. Luckily, no scientific studies exist to prove that tea is not healthy.

I would also love to be able to give definitive numbers about the levels of caffeine in these different teas, but the amount of caffeine varies too much—both from one plant to another and within the different teas—to offer any specifics. White teas likely have more caffeine than green teas or black teas because buds have more caffeine than mature leaves. And tea generally has about a third the caffeine of coffee. If you are trying to avoid caffeine, the best advice I can give is to drink herbal tea. Tea makers can remove caffeine from tea by rinsing the leaves in either ethyl acetate or supercritical carbon dioxide—liquid CO_2. Both are safe, but both leach out the more nuanced flavors along with the stimulant.

For tea connoisseurs, caffeine and polyphenols each affect a tea's flavor along with sugars, amino acids, and fatty acids. Sugars obviously make the tea sweet. Fatty acids provide tea with many of its aromas. Amino acids influence body, giving teas their relative brothiness, or *umami*. One amino acid in particular, called "L-theanine" ("theanine" for short), seems to create the most mouth-filling qualities. Japanese tea makers frequently speak of the favorable theanine levels in their best teas. Theanine has also been increasingly studied for its ability to soothe the brain and enhance concentration, making tea a gentler stimulant than coffee. Caffeine, an alkaloid, gives tea a mildly bitter bite. Polyphenols furnish tea with its tannic qualities, its relative astringency or briskness. Two have a particularly strong effect: EGCG, or epigallocatechin-3-gallate, a smooth-tasting polyphenol; and EC, or epicatechin, a harsher, grassy-tasting molecule. Spring teas taste particularly well rounded and mellow because they have the most EGCG and the least EC. Spring teas have different names in different countries: Qing Ming teas in China; Senchas in Japan; First Flush teas in Darjeeling.

In summer, the plants slow their growth, digging in for the heat and the assault of late-season insects. Japanese Banchas plucked in May and June taste grassy and thin compared with early-spring Senchas because they have about a third fewer amino acids and a much higher proportion of EC to EGCG. Second Flush Darjeelings and later-season oolongs like Bai Hao have far less glucose and fewer amino acids than their earlier-season equivalents. Makers of both teas compensate for the nutrient loss by allowing insects to attack them before harvesting. The plant reacts by producing a defensive compound with a lovely fruity aroma evocative of Muscat grapes.

To ensure the most flavors, tea makers have also developed a dizzying number of tea varietals, each with differing levels of the six chemical compounds. Almost all the pure teas in this book have been bred from two parent varietals: *Camellia sinensis* var. *sinensis*, a small-leafed variety indigenous to China; and *Camellia sinensis* var. *assamica*, a larger-leafed type native to Assam. From these two, tea makers have developed hundreds of cultivars. The exquisite Chinese breed *Da Bai* ("big white") produces extra-large, glucose-packed buds, perfect for white teas and tippy black teas. The Japanese cultivar *yabukita* grows in 90 percent of that country's tea gardens, because of its above-average levels of amino acids and relatively low levels of polyphenols. The black teas Keemun (China) and New Vithanakande (Sri Lanka) both get their chocolaty flavors in part from cultivars with extra amino acids.

After choosing the tea cultivar and the timing of the harvest, tea makers can also control the levels of compounds in tea—and therefore the tea's flavor—by gathering the leaves by hand. The finest teas also come from the very youngest leaves. Tea plants grow by sending out buds—incipient leaves shaped like spears that unfurl into young leaves, then mature. The youngest leaves on the plant are called "leafsets," consisting of a bud and its adjoining two leaves. These leafsets are loaded with nutrients to feed and protect the sprouts as they grow. Fully mature leaves contain comparatively few nutrients, since they send whatever they photosynthesize into the roots for storage. Mechanical harvesters cannot distinguish between leafsets and mature leaves; like crude hedge clippers, they merely shear the bushes of their outer layer. As a result, machine-harvested teas often taste dull and insipid. Most of the teas in this book were gathered by hand. It is meticulous work. Harvesters often wear gloves affixed with razor blades to snip off the leafsets one at a time, their fingers flying from branch to branch as they work their way down the bushes, gently storing the cut leaves in straw hampers as they work.

WITHERING

For all the work involved in harvesting it, freshly plucked tea tastes like bitter grass. Its hundreds of flavors don't begin to emerge until tea makers go to work to draw them out. As I've said, these flavors exist in the plant to defend it against attack. The first line of defense emerges right after the leaves have been plucked. Cut off from the roots, the leaves begin to lose moisture and nutrients. In an effort to feed themselves, the leaves break down starches into glucose and proteins into amino acids. In what scientists believe is an attempt to alert the rest of the plant that they are in distress, the leaves also transform fatty acids into aromatic compounds. These alerts are the first flavors to emerge, in this process called "withering," or dehydration, as tea makers let the leaves go limp.

The longer the leaves wither, the more aromas the final tea yields. Green teas wither only over the short trip between the field and the factory, just long enough to generate some of the lemony, grassy scents of linalools and hexanols. Oolongs and black teas wither much longer. Assam CTC teas are among the least aromatic black teas, as they wither very briefly; the humidity of tropical Assam makes dehydration nearly impossible.

On the opposite end of the spectrum, high-mountain oolongs, First Flush Darjeelings, and some high-grown Ceylons wither for several hours more—not just to provoke the aromas, but also to dry out the leaves and concentrate the compounds. Over so much time, fatty acids continue to degrade into yet more aromatic compounds like the geranium-scented geraniol and jasmine-scented methyl jasmonate. The aromatic compound methyl salicylate gives Uva Highlands Ceylon black tea its remarkable minty aroma. In addition to fatty acid degradation, in black teas and darker oolongs, which continue to wither as they oxidize, the pigment carotene starts to degrade into the aromatic compounds ionones, damascones, and damascenones, forming delicious fruity aromas reminiscent of apricots, peaches, and honey.

The scent of withering tea is incomparable—fresh and floral, far more vibrant than the final scents of brewed tea. Like a tea man's perfume counter, tea factories at the peak of harvest throb with aromas of lemon, jasmine, and apricot. I love to walk through them, smelling handfuls of the withering leaves.

❊ FIXING ❊

Makers of green teas bring all this aromatic activity to a halt when they "fix" the leaves, cooking them to keep them green. In the fruit and vegetable world, this reaction is called "enzymatic browning" and affects a host of ingredients including bananas, avocados, potatoes, and apples. If you slice open a potato, within a few minutes the exposed flesh will begin to darken. If you cook the potato, it will remain white. Tea makers similarly rapidly increase the leaves' internal temperature to 160 degrees Fahrenheit, deactivating the enzyme polyphenol oxidase, or PPO, that would otherwise turn them brown. (Another way to deactivate PPO is to deprive the enzyme of water, which it also needs to perform its duties. Uva

Highlands Ceylon tea and First Flush Darjeelings desiccate so severely after harvest that they undergo what's called a "hard wither," drying out in heated troughs to such an extent that they become partially fixed, like green teas.)

The fixing method impacts the tea's final taste. Imagine the difference between a steamed potato wedge and a browned, roasted one and you have a sense of the difference. Japanese green-tea makers steam their leaves in tunnels, giving the teas the more assertive, vegetal flavors of steamed spinach. Since World War II, some Japanese tea makers have begun steaming the leaves twice as long, for up to a minute instead of the traditional thirty seconds. The increase may seem slight, but it results in an even more assertive tea.

Certain Chinese green teas like Bi Lo Chun and Lung Ching have the lighter, slightly sweeter flavors of toasted nuts and steamed bok choy in part because Chinese tea makers sear the leaves over woks. The much hotter pans and ovens trigger what chemists call "the Maillard reaction." Named for Louis-Camille Maillard, the French chemist who first studied it at the turn of the last century, the reaction creates pyrroles, pyrazines, and other compounds tasting of baked peaches, roasted nuts, and similar baked or roasted flavors. A form of nonenzymatic browning, the Maillard reaction also darkens the teas somewhat.

Woks and ovens also give Chinese green teas a slightly wider range of aromas. Leaves reach 160 degrees Fahrenheit almost instantaneously when they are steamed, but they can take several minutes to heat up in a wok or a hot oven. Until they are fixed, the leaves continue to wither, producing yet more aromatic compounds. A comparison of the aromas in a Japanese Sencha and a Chinese wok-fired green tea shows that the Sencha has more lemony linalools, while the wok-fired tea has more carroty beta ionones and neriols, floral aromas more common to oolongs, which wither for a much longer period. Although Chinese green teas have nowhere near the aroma concentration of oolongs, they do have a slightly wider spectrum of scents than Japanese green teas.

ROLLING

After green teas have been fixed, and before black teas darken, tea makers roll the leaves to give them their lovely shapes. Once done by hand but now performed mainly by machine, rolling transforms the flat leaves into mesmerizing twists, coils, balls, or spears. In general, lightly rolled teas have mellower and gentler flavors, while leaves rolled with greater pressure break up into smaller pieces and form brews that are more brisk and intense. Chinese tea makers have invented innumerable balletlike hand movements over the centuries to create dozens of leaf shapes. In the 1880s, the British developed rolling machines that saved labor but made far less distinctive shapes and less refined teas.

OXIDATION

Where rolling gives green tea leaves their lovely shapes, with oolongs and black teas it also provokes the reaction that darkens the leaves. Oolongs and black teas are not fixed green but are allowed to darken through a process called "oxidation." In the tea world, for centuries this process was mistakenly called "fermentation," on the assumption that yeasts or bacteria were involved. In fact, the reaction involves only polyphenols and oxygen.

In a healthy tea leaf, polyphenols reside in "vacuoles," small chambers inside the plant cells, ready to defend the leaf against damage from insects and other hazards. If insects munch on the cells, or strong winds bruise the leaves as they rub against one another, or a tea maker macerates a leaf during the rolling process, the vacuoles also break, releasing the polyphenols into the cells' cytoplasm. In the cytoplasm, the polyphenols encounter the enzyme polyphenol oxidase, or PPO. In green teas, this enzyme does nothing, as it gets deactivated when the leaves are fixed—heated to 160 degrees Fahrenheit to render the enzyme inoperable. In oolongs and black teas, however, PPO reacts with the polyphenols and oxygen to form brown-colored compounds. In nature, these polyphenols are thought to deter further attack by giving the insects a stomachache. Luckily for tea drinkers, polyphenols are delicious as well as lovely to behold. In tea, there are two principal types of polyphenols, each with its own flavor and color. Golden, brisk theaflavins are the first to emerge. Later, thearubigins develop, mellower and with a lovely copper hue. The slower the oxidation, the more thearubigins, the gentler the teas.

Oolongs oxidize more slowly than other teas. As a result, they have the most complex, mellow flavors. Oolongs start to oxidize when they wither, because tea makers gently fluff the leaves on tarps in the sun. This fluffing qualifies as a very light rolling, triggering oxidation along the edges of the leaves. Indeed, the gentle agitation is what gives oolong leaves their characteristic red tinge. With a head start on oxidation, the edges turn a darker red than the rest of the leaf. After withering, the leaves are rolled incrementally, in an elaborate stop-and-start oxidation that lasts for six hours or more. This gradual oxidation prolongs the withering, allowing for the creation of yet more aromatic compounds. The final flavors and aromas depend entirely on the amount of time the oolongs are given to wither and oxidize. Of the nine oolongs in this book, the first four oxidize only roughly 25 percent. They contain high concentrations of linalool, methyl jasmonate, and indole and thus have the citrus and floral aromas of lime, jasmine, and gardenia. The final five oxidize between 40 and 75 percent and develop more of the apricot and peach flavors typical of carotenoid degradation, the later-stage transformation of the pigment carotene into the apricotlike compounds ionones, damascones, and damascenones.

Chinese black teas share many of these apricot notes. Though they oxidize more quickly than oolongs because of stronger rolling, they still oxidize slowly enough to produce sweet, mellow thearubigin-rich teas. The oxidation is slowed not by interruption, but by limiting the leaves' access to oxygen. First tea makers roll the leaves very gently, keeping them as whole as possible so that most of the polyphenols stay in their vacuoles. Then they pile the rolled leaves into deep, finely woven bamboo baskets. They leave them there for hours, covered with cloth, so oxygen reaches the leaves only at a trickle. The result is a soft, nuanced tea with full, rounded body.

British Legacy Teas share a briskness that comes from being oxidized very quickly. Likely because the British have long preferred a brisk tea, tea makers in the former British colonies roll their leaves into much finer particles. They then spread the particles in thin layers, often blown with heated air, which maximizes their exposure to oxygen. Orthodox British Legacy Teas are allowed to oxidize longer and more slowly, so they have more complex aromas.

In contrast, British Legacy CTC teas are the most astringent of all, as they oxidize virtually instantaneously. CTC stands for "crush, tear, and curl," the three stages of the "rolling," or crushing, process: The leaves are not rolled but pulverized, crushed through a fine sieve to tear into tiny shreds that curl into fine pellets. These pellets pass along a conveyor belt under powerful blowers; within the space of one hundred feet and a few hours, the pellets have switched, chameleonlike, from bright green to a flat, dull brown. These teas have almost no thearubigins; their tannic theaflavins make them robustly brisk and mouth-puckering. These teas taste so good with milk because the dairy proteins bind with the tannic compounds to soften them.

While oxidation turns buds gold, it darkens mature tea leaves almost to black. The source of the darker color is chlorophyll, which degrades during oxidation to murky brown pheophytins and pheophorbides. Buds contain very little chlorophyll, and what little they have dissolves during withering. For this reason, oxidation of buds reveals only the golden and coppery colors of degraded polyphenols.

⚹ FERMENTATION ⚹

Until recently, the process of oxidation was thought to be fermentation. Up until the mid-1900s, tea makers assumed that yeasts and bacteria turned tea black by converting sugars to alcohol the same way wines and breads ferment. In fact, only puerh tea ferments, and the puerh-making process is such a closely guarded secret that it's hard to know exactly how this happens. But we can speculate: As the teas age, sugars within the leaves are converted to monoterpenoids, which in turn oxidize and degrade over the years into sesquiterpenoids. Sesquiterpenoid compounds have the earthy and camphor flavors that puerhs are known for.

⚹ FIRING ⚹

The final step in tea production, firing preserves teas by almost completely removing any remaining moisture. "Drying" would be a more accurate term; if the leaves' moisture is reduced to 3 percent, the tea is stable and no more chemical reactions can take place. It can then travel. In ancient China that meant to the next province; now it means anywhere around the globe.

Depending on how heavily it is done, firing can also profoundly affect a tea's flavor. Today, teas are commonly dried in ovens or woks. The Chinese originally dried tea over wood fires, which is how the drying process got its name. Over time, wood was replaced with charcoal, a more enduring and even source of heat. Today, the only teas still fired with wood smoke are the Chinese black tea Lapsang Souchong and the oolong Da Hong Pao. By far the majority of teas are dried in electric ovens. Before all the moisture is lost, the heat of the dryers can provoke the same Maillard reaction that sweetens Chinese green teas. The Maillard reaction provokes the formation of dimethylpyrazines, which make for the chocolate and cocoa notes in New Vithanakande Ceylon tea and Keemun Chinese black teas. It also bolsters the honey and malt qualities of Assams. The best teas have the finest roasted aromas because they have the most amino acids.

Firing can also take flavors away: Some of the floral aromas in green tea are too volatile to survive the heat of firing; *aracha,* or raw, unfired Japanese green tea, is often more aromatic than the finished version. In the last thirty years, as innovations in packaging materials have rendered heavy firings unnecessary, tea makers have begun experimenting with lighter and lighter firings, creating ever lighter and more aromatic teas. However, there is still a demand for old-school teas that have been heavily fired, just as there is still a market in the wine world for wines with an "oaked" flavor, even though technology has eliminated any practical need to store wine in oak barrels.

SORTING

After firing, tea makers sort the teas by leaf size by agitating the leaves through a series of screens. Whole leaves impart the fullest array of flavors; they are separated out first for the best-quality teas. The next smaller particles are called "brokens"; they make strong, brisk cups of tea. The smallest particles are called "fannings" and "dust." Fannings get their name from the fans that were once used to sort them: Before the age of machines, tea makers sorted the leaves by tossing them into the air from a large bamboo fan. The leaves light enough to blow off onto the floor were separated as fannings; the ones large enough to fall back into the fan were reserved as the best tea. Today, fannings and dust are set aside for teabags and instant teas. With only a few noted exceptions, all the teas in this book are whole-leaf teas.

APPENDIX

Tea Through Time: A Brief History

The history of tea is more complex and spectacular than I can convey here, and I heartily recommend that you draw on other sources to get to know the ways the commodity has shaped our world. To educate your palate, it helps to get down a few facts, if only to allow you to understand why tea comes in so many forms.

Trying to establish when tea was first made—and in what form—is like trying to establish in what year Hades built the underworld. Tea marketers have every incentive to mythologize, hardly any to be accurate, and it all began so long ago. As a Taiwanese tea broker once admitted to me, "Legend works much better than fact if you want to keep a customer at the counter. There's much more to talk about."

We can say for certain that tea first grew wild in the Himalayan foothills, in what today are parts of China and India. Humans first started drinking tea approximately five thousand years ago in the mountains of southwest China in what is now Yunnan province. The first harvesters merely toppled the trees in spring, before learning how to pluck the bushes continuously. The dried leaves were preserved in tightly compressed cakes.

Cultivated initially for its medicinal qualities, tea was consumed as a kind of bitter green leaf vegetable soup, primarily by practitioners of Taoism, Confucianism, and Buddhism. Simultaneously calming and stimulating, though also incredibly bitter, the crude beverage held devotees of all three religions in the ideal clear state of mind during their lessons and meditations. All three practices sprouted and flourished in China during the political turmoil of the latter end of the Zhou dynasty (1122–256 BC). Each school played an important role in the dissemination of tea from its mountain roots to the wider Asian continent, particularly Buddhism. As the religion spread eastward from the Himalayas into Japan and Southeast Asia, tea went with it. Monks cultivated the tea, creating the first methods of propagation and selling the beverage to support their monasteries. They also taught area farmers how to grow their beverage. In the ninth century AD, while China was enjoying a fad for steam-fixed green teas, Buddhists first brought tea to Japan from a monastery in China (see "Jin Shan," page 35). Three hundred years later, a Japanese monk named Eisai, who would found the Japanese arm of Zen Buddhism, brought over Chinese powdered green tea now known as Matcha.

Tea first flourished in Japan around the imperial capital of Kyoto. The great tea gardens still stand in Uji on the outskirts of the city, planted there to serve the emperor's court as well as the capital's magnificent Buddhist temples. The Japanese made their teas according to the fashion in China during the Song and Ming dynasties, when tea first made its way from China to Japan. The leaves were ground into a powder, whipped to a foamy froth in individual serving bowls, and passed around in an elaborate, formalized ritual that has come to be known as "the Japanese tea ceremony," first codified by Sen Rikyu in the late sixteenth century. Rikyu used the ritualized presentation of tea as a lesson in *wabi-sabi,* the observation and appreciation of everyday objects. For centuries, Matcha served according to these rituals was consumed mostly by royalty, then the warrior class of samurai, who adopted the contemplative philosophy aligned with the tea ceremony called Chado: "the Way of Tea." For the samurai, serving tea with full awareness provided physical and spiritual fulfillment, to both the giver and the receiver. Though the feudal government has long since fallen away, as a reflection of that smaller island's remarkable cultural stability, the nation continues to steam-fix its teas, many Japanese still drink powdered Matcha tea, and some still practice the tea ceremony.

Meanwhile, the far more turbulent nation of China established its own tradition of tea-making innovation. Tea became a truly national drink there in or around the third to fifth centuries AD, when it finally lost its bitterness. Tea makers realized that steaming the leaves after harvesting made the tea much more palatable—and popular. Tea soon commanded the attention of emperors, who began demanding the best teas as tribute teas. Having a tea selected as a tribute tea guaranteed tea makers a fortune. Competition for the emperor's attention proved a great incentive for the invention of new teas, a tradition of innovation that has lasted hundreds of years. As tea makers competed for imperial attention, white tea first emerged in the Song dynasty (960–1279); loose tea during the Ming dynasty (1368–1644); black tea and then oolongs in the early part of the Qing dynasty (1644–1911). Today, China still boasts the greatest variety of tea plant cultivars. The country's Tea Research Institute lists 650—almost twice as many teas as the number of cheeses in France. By comparison, 90 percent of Japanese tea farms grow one cultivar called *yabukita*. And while the Japanese still steam their teas, as the Chinese did 1,200 years ago, Chinese tea makers have long since abandoned steam for hot air, woks, and wood fires.

Tea did not arrive in the Western world until the seventeenth century. As the first and second Europeans to make landfall in South Asia, the Portuguese and later the Dutch brought back the first teas to Europe. Tea became popular among the British aristocracy in the eighteenth century, but it wasn't until the nineteenth century that the drink became indispensable to the British economy. Amid that century's industrialization, poor members of the working class used tea and milk as a cheap vehicle for that other recent colonial import, sugar. Tea became yet more popular in the later part of the nineteenth century when the British temperance movement promoted it as a substitute for alcohol. Some conspiracy theorists posit that the temperance movement was a creation of the East India Company, the largest corporation in history and for many decades holder of the monopoly on Great Britain's tea export business.

The East India Company's work in China, to the Eastern country's detriment, proved far from peaceable. With the benefit of hindsight, some of its actions seem downright despicable. Nonetheless, the rough turn of events ultimately proved beneficial to the world of tea: The East India Company's voracious need for the dried leaves led to an explosion in the number of varieties available to us today.

In the early 1800s, as Japan had closed its doors to international trade, China was the world's only source for tea. Thus, "all the tea in China" meant all the tea in the world. The Chinese guarded their tea-growing methods carefully: For over hundred years, the British believed green teas and black teas came from separate plants and read in their schoolbooks that the leaves were harvested by monkeys. (This misconception may account for the high number of Chinese teas whose names still include some allusion to primates, like the black tea Golden Monkey and the green tea Taiping HouKui, or Best Monkey Tea.)

By the mid-nineteenth century, the British were drinking more tea than they could pay the Chinese for. As part of a larger series of events, Great Britain sent industrial espionage agents who literally stole tea plants—as many as a few hundred—to see if they could be grown in their new colony of India. After much trial and error, by the end of the nineteenth century they had established immense plantations in the Indian substates of Darjeeling and Assam as well as the small island of Ceylon (now called Sri Lanka). Those same envoys who stole the plants also snuck into Chinese tea-making regions to observe their ancient methods of growing, harvesting, and shaping small batches of tea entirely by hand. The first British tea planters adopted these Chinese techniques but found they took too much time, labor, and money. So the British tea men, proud products of the Industrial Revolution, created more efficient, entirely mechanical ways to make teas, essentially inventing a new class of brew. These machine-harvested, machine-processed black teas appeared in heretofore unseen quantities, darker and brisker than any teas before them. They are discussed in "British Legacy Black Teas," page 121.

These new plantations proved such a success that by 1906, the British were buying from China only 5 percent of the tea they had bought thirty years before. All the tea in China was now, for the most part, stuck in China. In no small part because of this catastrophic collapse in trade, by 1927 the once flourishing state of China had collapsed into civil war, with a new Communist regime emerging as the victor. The Communists initially proved disastrous for China's teas, placing thousands of small farms under largely inept state management and then isolating the entire country under an international trade embargo after the Korean War. In retrospect, the world of tea in fact benefited from these years of isolation. China's ancient tea-making traditions survived intact, when they might otherwise have been sacrificed to modernization. Western plantation methods did a fine job making certain basic styles of black tea, but they would have ruined the refined ancient teas of China.

China's traditional methods were preserved as well on the island of Formosa (now Taiwan), a hundred miles across the straits from Fujian province, to which some tea growers immigrated in the mid-1800s to establish a flourishing tea industry. Today, Taiwan produces some extraordinary teas, discussed in the chapter on oolongs, page 75.

It is remarkable how long some things endure. Popular myth still holds that the world gets its teas from India and China by way of Great Britain. I frequently get asked if Harney & Sons is a British company, as if that were proof of our quality. The truth is when British tea companies were evicted from India and

Sri Lanka after World War II, the British brought tea to their colonies in Africa, primarily Kenya. Today, tea is grown in over thirty-five countries, including Indonesia, Turkey, and South Africa. Over 40 percent of the tea drunk in Great Britain comes from Kenya, while about 40 percent of the tea drunk in the United States is grown in Argentina. Most of those teas are destined for teabags (if not instant iced tea powder) and are not very good. The best teas available today—and with one Kenyan exception, all the teas in this book—come from Asia: China, Japan, and Taiwan, as well as what we now call the British Legacy Teas from the former colonies of India and Sri Lanka.

APPENDIX

Tea Sources

A s interest in tea grows, more and more tea importers and tea shops have emerged. Here are the suppliers I most admire and the ones I encourage you to visit while shopping for the teas in this book.

HARNEY & SONS FINE TEAS

This is the company I run with my father, John, and my brother Paul. We're honoredto supply teas to some of the finest restaurants, hotels, and tea drinkers in the world.

The Railroad Plaza
Main Street
Millerton, NY
800-TEA-TIME (832–8463)
www.harneyteas.com

IMPERIAL TEA COURT

Roy Fong runs several terrific Chinese tea rooms in the San Francisco area. He was the first one to point me down the road of great Chinese teas.

1411 Powell Street
San Francisco, CA 94133
800-567-5898
www.imperialtea.com

MARIAGE FRÈRES

Founded in 1854, Mariage Frères is the oldest tea company in France. In the early 1980s, the Mariage family sold the firm to Richard Bueno and Kitti Cha Sangmanee. The two have inspired me to great heights ever since.

35, rue du Bourg-Tibourg
75004 Paris
France
www.mariagefreres.com

NOTHING BUT TEA

Nigel Melican is a treasure to the world tea industry, both for his deep knowledge and for his commitment to helping emerging tea regions. He runs this UK Web site with his daughter.

www.nbtea.co.uk (online only)

RISHI TEA

Joshua Kaiser started in the tea business less than a decade ago, but he keeps me on my toes with his smart sourcing.

www.rishi-tea.com (online only)

UPTON TEA

Based in Massachusetts, Tom Eck supplies an encyclopedic variety of teas through his Web site.

www.uptontea.com (online only)

ACKNOWLEDGMENTS

Many people helped me put this book together, especially since it was my first literary endeavor. First I want to thank my father, John. Without him there would be no book, as there would be no Harney & Sons. He introduced me to this special little world of tea, which has been my obsession for twenty years. I hope I can pass his enthusiasm on to the next generation of Harneys. James Norwood Pratt was an inspiration; I always enjoy his command of the language. Marcus Wulf of Germany's HamburgerTeeHandel tea brokerage firm has been a fellow traveler in tea for many years. Few in the world have his experience. He has been invaluable to this book, extraordinarily generous with his knowledge and contacts. He quizzed tea producers across the globe about current production methods for me. I tip my cup to him.

Other experts have proven indispensable: Tsuyoshi Sugimoto may be the most astute observer of Japanese teas. I always listen to his sage advice about Japan's teas, past and present. Wang Shengdu is an expert on all the wonderful teas of Fujian province and hosted some long trips around that beautiful area of China. Lu Shun Yong has worked with the green teas of Zhejiang province for many years, yet he still looks so young. Shao Hui knows the back roads of Anhui province and makes a wonderful Keemun Mao Feng. Steve He almost gave away the secret of yellow teas from Junshan in Hunan province, but thought twice. Ashok Lohia of Chamong Group and his assistant, Ajay

ACKNOWLEDGMENTS

Kichlu, make some of the best Darjeelings in that region, and gave me great insight into Darjeeling production. Also quite helpful with current conditions in India were Subrata Basu of Jayshree and Soumitra Banerjee of the venerable Goodricke. Amit Kumar Sen of Godfrey Phillips India and Krishan Kaytal of J. Thomas & Co. both elucidated the Calcutta brokers' viewpoint on Indian teas. Lalin Fernando and Amitha Wijiskera shed light on the delicious world of Ceylon teas. The intricacies of Taiwanese oolongs were revealed to me over the years (and many lovely cups of tea) by Hsiang Bin and George Shu. Peter Davies, a professor of plant biology at Cornell University, helped me articulate what really happens inside green tea leaves. After two decades in the tea trade, there are quite a few more people I would love to include here; I appreciate them and have passed on their knowledge with this book as best I could.

As much as I have learned about tea, however, turning all my knowledge into a book required some alchemy. Ileene Smith thought I could be more than her child's hockey coach and introduced me to my agent, Melanie Jackson. Melanie saw the potential of this book, and I am thankful for her sage advice and her love of Japanese teas. I am so grateful to Ann Godoff and her talented associates at The Penguin Press: Lindsay Whalen, Claire Vaccaro, and Tracy Locke. Most first-time authors do not have the honor of working with such a tremendous publishing team.

No one could ask for more, yet I got more. Emily Kaiser has been a treasure. I am grateful to Dana Cowin of *Food & Wine* for allowing her to do this project. Emily made my thoughts and words into the book it is today. What's more, her knowledge of the food world and her organizational skills made this book immeasurably better. It was a joy to teach her about tea.

BIBLIOGRAPHY

Ball, Samuel. *An Account of the Cultivation and Manufacture of Tea in China*. London: Longman, Brown, Green and Longmans, 1848.

Chow, Kit, and Ione Kramer. *All the Tea in China*. San Francisco: China Books and Perodicals, 1990.

Dekker, Marcel. *Flavor of Tea*. Philadelphia: Food Reviews International, 1995.

Eden, T. *Tea*. London: Longmans, Green and Co. Ltd, 1965.

Etherington, Dan, and Keith Forster. *The Structural Transformation of Taiwan's Tea Industry*. Montreal: World Development, 1992.

———. *Green Gold*. Hong Kong: Oxford University Press, 1993.

Evans, John. *Tea in China*. Westport, CT: Greenwood Press, 1992.

BIBLIOGRAPHY

Fernando, Maxwell. *The Story of Ceylon Tea.* Colombo: Mlesna (Ceylon) Limited, 2000.

Firestein, Stuart. *How the Olfactory System Makes Sense of Scents.* London: Nature Publishing Group, 2002.

Forrest, Denys. *A Hundred Years of Ceylon Tea.* London: Chatto & Windus, 1967.

———. *Tea for the British.* London: Chatto & Windus, 1973.

Fortune, Robert. *A Journey to the Tea Countries of China.* London: John Murray, 1852.

Gardella, Robert. *Harvesting Mountains.* Berkeley: University of California Press, 1994.

———. *Qing Administration of the Tea Trade.* Edited by Jane Kate Leonard. Ithaca, NY: East Asia Program, 1992.

Graham, Patricia. *Tea for the Sages: The Art of Sencha.* Honolulu: University of Hawaii Press, 1998.

Guotu, Zhuang. *Tea, Silver, Opium and War.* Xiamen: Xiamen University Press, 1994.

Harler, C. R. *The Culture and Marketing of Tea.* London: Oxford University Press, 1934.

Jain, N. K., ed. *Global Advances in Tea Science.* New Delhi: Aravali Books International (P) Ltd., 1999.

Kamp, David. *The United States of Arugula.* New York: Broadway Books, 2006.

Leffingwell, John. *Olfaction*. www.leffingwell.com, 2008.

Liu, Tong. *Chinese Tea*. Beijing: China Intercontinental Press, 2005.

Lu, Yu. *Classic of Tea*. Translated by Francis Ross Carpenter, Boston: Little, Brown & Co. 1974.

MacFarlane, Alan and Iris. *Green Gold*. London: Random House, 2003.

Mauler, Jean Marie. *Connaitre et aimer le thé*. Geneva: Editions Nicholas Junod, 1999.

Mintz, Sidney W. *Sweetness and Power: The Place of Sugar in Modern History*. New York: Penguin Books, 1985.

Moxham, Roy. *Tea: Addiction, Exploitation, and Empire*. New York: Carroll & Graf, 2004.

Pollan, Michael. *The Botany of Desire*. New York: Random House, 2001.

Pratt, James Norwood. *New Tea Lover's Treasury*. San Francisco: Publishing Technology Associates, 1999.

Rowe, David J., ed. *Chemistry and Technology of Flavors and Fragrances*. Oxford: Blackwell Publishing Ltd, 2005.

Schuh, Christian, and Peter Schieberle. "Characterization of the Key Aroma Compounds in the Beverage Prepared from Darjeeling Black Tea." *Journal of Agricultural and Food Chemistry* 54 (2006): 916–924.

Standage, Tom. *A History of the World in 6 Glasses*. New York: Walker & Company, 2005.

Turin, Luca. *The Secret of Scent*. New York: Ecco, 2006.

Wang, Ling. *Chinese Tea Culture*. Beijing: Foreign Language Press, 2000.

Wilkinson, Sophie. "Plants to Bugs: Buzz Off!" *Chemical & Engineering News* (2001).

Willson, K. C., and M. N. Clifford, eds. *Tea: Cultivation to Consumption*. London: Chapman & Hall, 1992.

Ukers, William H. *All About Tea*. New York: The Tea and Coffee Trade Journal Company, 1935.

INDEX

ABOUT THE AUTHORS

Michael Harney has been the tea buyer and blender of Harney & Sons for twenty years. He travels to Asia and meets with tea producers from all the major tea countries, looking for the season's best teas. A graduate of Cornell University's School of Hotel Administration, he lives with his wife and their three sons in Salisbury, Connecticut.

Emily Kaiser is an associate food editor at *Food & Wine*. She lives in New York.